RAILWAYS
AT THE ZENITH OF STEAM
1920–40

Railways of the World in Colour

RAILWAYS
AT THE ZENITH OF STEAM
1920–40

by
O. S. NOCK

Illustrated by
CLIFFORD and WENDY MEADWAY

LONDON
BLANDFORD PRESS

First published in 1970

Printed in Great Britain by
Richard Clay (The Chaucer Press), Ltd., Bungay, Suffolk

INTRODUCTION

The first years of the twentieth century were an age of railway pre-eminence all over the world. Men were travelling faster than at any time previously in the history of civilization, and it was by trains, hauled by steam locomotives, that they were doing so. Competition with railways was arising on a limited scale in many areas. Electric tramways were being laid in the streets of many great cities and indeed in smaller townships. The petrol-engine motor car was developing; men were learning to fly, but up to the year 1914 the supremacy of railways was absolute in all the most highly developed countries of the world. In developing countries the few pioneer railways were virtually the only means of long-distance transport.

By the year 1920 all was beginning to change. The urgent needs of wartime had acted as a spur to the rapid developments of road transport in petrol-engined vehicles, and of aircraft; in Great Britain in particular the public was quick to appreciate that road motor services, however uncomfortable at first, were in many cases more convenient than railways for local transport, while enterprising carriers gave what was virtually a door-to-door service of goods. At first it seemed that railways in many parts of the world were a little slow in realizing the seriousness of the new competition that was springing up; but then they began to gear themselves to the need for more competitive services, and with this came the first steps to 'cash in' on what was the most important asset of railways—speed.

This book covers the period when many enterprising developments were in progress all over the world. In locomotive design American steam power grew to colossal proportions. Much of this was to provide little except brute strength for hauling immense loads. Refinements of earlier years, such as the use of multicylindered engine units and compound expansion, were discarded in favour of making everything as simple as possible and readily accessible for maintenance purposes without the need for going over a pit. Even the largest engines of the non-articulated type had no more than two cylinders. Design skill lay in the direction of producing working parts that would withstand the stresses set up in continuous all-out working for hours on end. Outstanding engines in this category that we illustrate are the Sante Fé '3771' class, and the New York Central 'Niagara', both having the 4-8-4 wheel arrangement.

In Great Britain throughout this period the tendency in top-line express passenger power was just the reverse. Refinements in design to secure economy in fuel were numerous. Not one of the four main-line railways used two-cylinder locomotives for the principal express workings, and in studying this trend it must be appreciated that in Great Britain the railways were constantly labouring under the handicap of being pioneers; that if they had been following, instead of leading, bridges, tunnels, and other lineside structures would have been built to carry heavier, wider, and taller locomotives and carriages. Despite these handicaps, however, the skill of British railway engineers in all branches was such that many outstanding achievements in speed and train services were achieved, on a railway system that operated one of the most dense traffics to be found anywhere in the world. Some of the fastest trains of all had to be routed through this very crowded network.

In this book we see not only the locomotives that ran such services but also examples of the coaching stock, and the signals that regulated their safe running. One thing is noticeable, in comparison with other countries, and that is the size of the freight locomotives. Only one company, the London and North Eastern, introduced a really large engine for mineral traffic. The continued use of loose-coupled, unbraked goods trains precluded any acceleration of service, and longer trains than eighty or ninety wagons were an embarrassment. Consequently, locomotives of traditional proportions were adequate, and the two large 'P1' class 2-8-2s of the L.N.E.R. were larger than were really needed.

Although the British developments in locomotive design were notably successful, and produced much spectacular running as well as an outstanding degree of reliability in general service, it was in France that the greatest advances in steam locomotive practice were made, following the rebuilding by Monsieur André Chapelon of certain elderly 'Pacifics' of the Paris–Orleans Railway. The larger-wheeled variety was rebuilt as a 'Pacific', which in France went by the name of the 'P.O. Transformation'; and a 'transformation' certainly Chapelon had wrought. At the same time the smaller-wheeled engines were rebuilt as 4-8-0s. The interesting feature, in contrast to both British and American contemporary practice, was that the compound expansion was retained, with all its associated complications. Chapelon and those who followed his lead sought high thermal efficiency above all else. There was no question at that stage in French railway history of running at spectacularly high speeds, because with only the slightest exceptions there was an overall speed limit of 120 km. per hr. (74½ m.p.h.) throughout the country.

French policy in design was possible only because of the unique standards of main-

tenance that then prevailed. Locomotives had their own drivers and firemen; the drivers were all skilled mechanics, and looked after their machines with the diligence and care bestowed on a highly cherished and personally serviced motor car. At the same period in railway history many of the crack American express locomotives were engaged on duties that took them in a single run half across the continent; they would be handled by six, seven, or eight different crews successively in the one journey, and at many of the stops they would be routine-serviced by men whose only tool seemed to be a grease-gun. British practice in many areas was a half-way house between the two. Single manning was rare, but on the hardest duties selected links of engines and men worked in rotation, and the results were closely watched.

Towards the end of the period of this book it was becoming evident that steam had reached its limit in certain areas, and its replacement by newer forms of traction was beginning. To some extent this was governed by economic conditions relating to fuel supply. It was no longer economic to ship coal across the South Atlantic Ocean to be used as a locomotive fuel in Argentina. Electric traction gave many advantages, particularly in securing rapid acceleration, yet at the same time political upheavals, local wars, and civil commotion in far countries could seriously affect fuel supplies. Many countries reconsidered their motive-power policy in the light of the fuel that was indigenously available. In France, for example, the Paris, Lyons, and Mediterranean Railway no longer used its own colliers to fetch high-quality bituminous coal from South Wales; locomotives were adapted to use the qualities available in France, and on certain sections of the line to burn oil.

With these changed economics came also the realization that railway services must be intensively advertised. The great increase in civil air travel suggested to many sophisticated patrons that railways—particularly steam—were out of date. The railways had to show they were 'with it', and one facet of publicity took the form of streamlining locomotives and coaching stock. Some interesting and quaint examples of locomotive streamlining are illustrated in this book. It was claimed that such adornments had their practical value, as well as creating publicity. But the reduction of air resistance and the slight reduction in coal consumption that resulted were perhaps more than off-set by making the working parts inaccessible, and bearings and such like were more likely to heat. Streamlining proved little more than a passing phase, but it was a picturesque one while it lasted.

In the period under review not a great deal of change took place in passenger rolling stock. British designs were usually the most colourful, while the coaches of the principal countries on the continent of Europe were, externally, most unrelievedly dull. With the streamlined locomotives came a few gay new colour schemes, particularly in the U.S.A.; but generally speaking, carriage design remained traditional. There was nevertheless a marked change in the type of rail-motorcars, or railcars, as they came to be known. From the car propelled by a miniature steam locomotive on the same chassis the pure railcar began to emerge, sometimes steam propelled, as in the Clayton and Sentinel types, but also in diesel and electrically propelled cars. It must be admitted, however, that the potentialities of attractive, speedy railcars for local services, particularly in scenic districts, were not exploited, and the cumbrous method of running ordinary locomotive-hauled trains of standard coaching stock remained. The German 'glass' train, operating from Munich, was a most notable exception.

Concurrently with the changes in locomotive practice and style there commenced also a change in signalling methods. In former days the great arrays of semaphore signals made a most picturesque setting to many a busy railway scene. In the 1920s the immense advantage of colour-light signals was gradually realized, and although not adopted extensively at that date, the standards were established. The pictures in this book show some of the stages passed through in the British development of this art. Although the U.S.A. was first in the field with the introduction of light signals, British practice was developed into an extremely simple code which has proved adequate for the far faster and more intense main-line train services of today. On the continent of Europe the introduction of light signals came generally at a time later than in Great Britain, and some of the codes of practice worked out were considerably more complicated. In these days, when the red, amber, and green lights of road-traffic signals are so familiar to so many, it is sometimes imagined that the colour-light signals now being so extensively installed on British Railways are a derivative of the road signals. As a matter of historical fact the first day colour-light signals on a British railway were installed six years earlier than the first road-traffic signals; the latter, which were installed in Piccadilly, London, at the junction of St. James's Street were of purely railway type. The design was subsequently modified extensively to render it suitable generally for road conditions.

All in all, the period from 1920 to 1940 on railways all over the world was an exciting and fruitful one.

1 **Great Western Railway**: the 'King George V' in the U.S.A.

2 **Northern Railway of France**: the 'Collin' super-Pacific

EXPRESS LOCOMOTIVE VARIETY

GERMANY

3 **German State Railways**: a standard 'Pacific' locomotive.

BELGIUM

4 **Belgian National Railways**: a Flamme 'Pacific'.

5 **Great Indian Peninsular Railway**: 4-6-0 express passenger locomotive of 1922.

6 **Chicago and North Western Railway**: Class 'E' 'Pacific' locomotive of 1921.

SWITZERLAND

7 **Swiss Federal Railways**: a 4-cylinder compound 4–6–0 for the Gotthard Line.

SWEDEN

8 **Swedish State Railways**: Class 'F' express passenger 'Pacific'.

9 **Southern Railway (England)**: the 'King Arthur' class 4–6–0.

10 **Austrian State Railways**: 4–8–0 general service locomotive.

MAIN LINE CARRIAGES

ENGLAND

11 **Great Western Railway**: 70ft. bogie corridor carriage of 1923.

ITALY

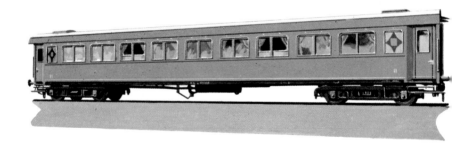

12 **Italian State Railways**: corridor carriage.

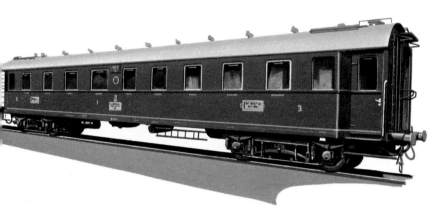

13　**German State Railways**: corridor carriage.

14　**Rhodesia Railways**: first class sleeping car.

LOCAL TANK LOCOMOTIVES

EIRE

15   **Great Southern Railway (Eire)**: 2-6-2 tank engine.

HOLLAND

16   **Netherlands Railways**: 4-6-4 tank engine.

17   **Czecho-Slovakian Railways**: 2-8-4 tank engine.

18   **Bengal Nagpur Railway**: 2-8-2 tank engine.

MAMMOTH CONTINENTAL LOCOMOTIVES

AUSTRIA

19 **Austrian State Railways**: 2-8-4 express locomotive.

FRANCE

20 **Eastern Railway of France**: 4-8-2 compound express locomotive.

21 **Paris, Lyons and Mediterranean Railway**: 4-8-2
compound express locomotive.

22 **Spanish National Railway (RENFE)**: ex-Norte
4-8-2 express locomotive.

23 **Pennsylvania Railroad**: the 'K4s' Pacific.

24 **Baltimore and Ohio**: Class EL-5A 2-8-8-0 simple articulated locomotive.

25 **Atchison, Topeka & Sante Fé Railroad**: 2-10-4 express freight engine.

26 **Lehigh and New England Railroad**: an 0-8-0 'switcher'.

27　**New South Wales Government Railways**: the 'C36'
class express passenger 4–6–0.

28　**New South Wales Government Railways**: the 'D57'
heavy goods 4–8–2.

29 **New South Wales Government Railways**: the 'C32'
    class 4-6-0 express passenger engine.

30 **New South Wales Government Railways**: the 'C35'
    class 4-6-0.

GREAT BRITAIN

31 **London, Midland and Scottish Railway**: 12-wheeled
dining and kitchen car.

ENGLAND

32 **Southern Railway (England)**: Pullman car.

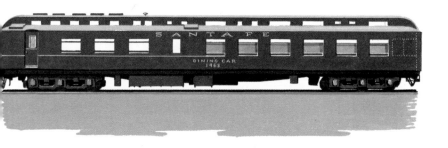

33 **Atchison, Topeka & Sante Fé Railroad**: dining car of trans–continental express.

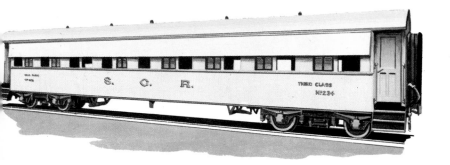

34 **Sudan Government Railways**: third class carriage.

LOCOMOTIVES OF SOUTHERN AFRICA

RHODESIA

35 **Rhodesia Railways**: 4-8-2 passenger and mail engine.

SOUTH AFRICA

36 **South African Railways**: the 'MJ' class Mallet
articulated 2-6-6-0 compound.

37 **Benguela Railway**: 4–8–0 general service locomotive.

38 **South African Railways**: the pioneer Beyer Garratt locomotive.

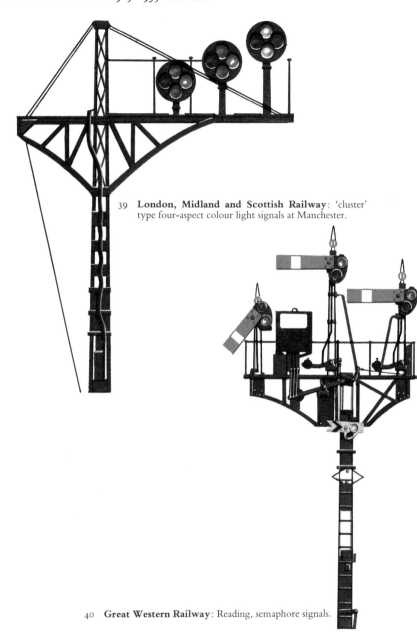

39 **London, Midland and Scottish Railway**: 'cluster' type four-aspect colour light signals at Manchester.

40 **Great Western Railway**: Reading, semaphore signals.

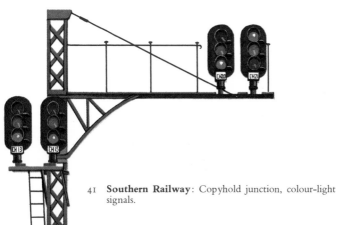

41 **Southern Railway**: Copyhold junction, colour-light signals.

42 **Great Western Railway**: Cardiff, 'searchlight' signals.

ENGLAND

43 **Great Western Railway**: the 'Castle' class 4-cylinder
4-6-0.

FRANCE

44 **Northern Railway of France**: a Chapelon 4-6-2
(ex-P.O. Midi).

U.S.A.

45 **Pennsylvania Railroad**: the 'Mla' 4-8-2 mixed traffic
locomotive.

U.S.A.

46 **Chicago, Milwaukee, St. Paul & Pacific Railroad**:
record-breaking 4-6-4 express locomotive.

GIANT ARTICULATED LOCOMOTIVES

INDIA

47 **Bengal Nagpur Railway**: the Class 'N' 4-8-0+0-8-4
Beyer Garratt engine.

U.S.A.

48 **Chesapeake and Ohio**: 2-8-8-2 simple articulated
freight engine.

FREIGHT AND MIXED TRAFFIC TYPES

ENGLAND

49 **Great Western Railway**: 2–8–0 heavy mineral locomotive.

INDIA

50 **Great Indian Peninsular Railway**: 2–8·0 heavy freight
locomotive.

51 **South African Railways**: the '15A' mixed traffic 4-8-2 locomotive.

52 **Nizam's Guaranteed State Railway**: 2-8-0 mixed traffic locomotive.

53 **International Sleeping Car Company**: a European standard sleeping car.

SIAM

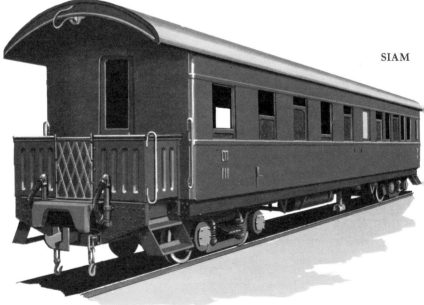

54 **Royal State Railways of Siam** (now Thailand): second and third class composite carriage.

55 **London and North Eastern Railway**: tourist train buffet car.

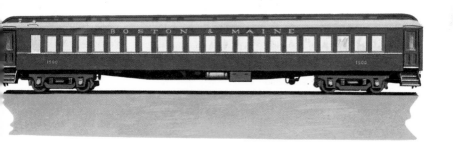

56 **Boston and Maine Railroad**: standard passenger car.

U.S.A.

57 **Chesapeake and Ohio**: bogie coal car.

ENGLAND

58 **Great Western Railway**: 120-ton trolley wagon.

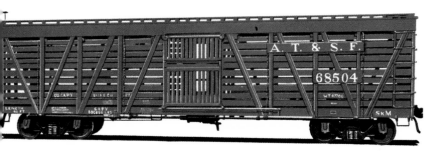

59 **Atchison, Topeka & Sante Fé Railroad**: double-deck stock car.

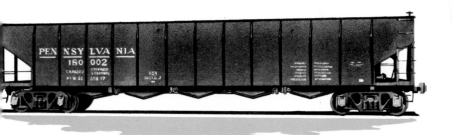

60 **Pennsylvania Railroad**: 85-ton hopper car.

GREAT BRITAIN

61 **London, Midland and Scottish Railway**: Aisgill
signal box.

GREAT BRITAIN

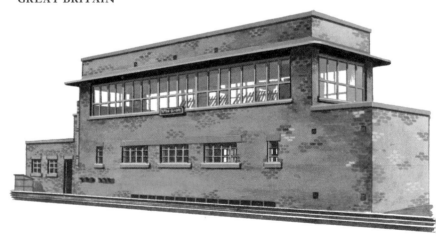

62 **London, Midland and Scottish Railway**: Toton
Marshalling Yard signal box.

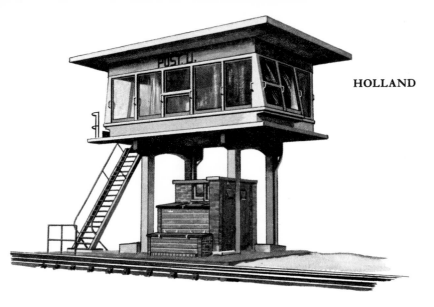

HOLLAND

63 **Delft 'Post U'** Dutch signal box.

ENGLAND

64 **Southern Railway**: Bickley Junction signal box.

LARGE ARTICULATED LOCOMOTIVES

SOUTH AFRICA

65 **South African Railways**: the giant 'MH' class 2-6-6-2 Mallet articualted compound.

SOUTH AFRICA

66 **South African Railways**: the 'GL' class 4-8-2+2-8-4 Beyer-Garratt freight engine.

67 **Kenya and Uganda Railway**: the 'EC2' class Beyer
Garratt locomotive.

68 **Southern Pacific Lines**: the cab-in-front 4–8–8–2 of
1928.

69 **Great Northern Railway of Ireland**: 3-cylinder compound 4-4-0 locomotive.

70 **Great Southern Railway (Eire)**: 2-cylinder 4-6-0 express locomotive.

71 **London, Midland and Scottish Railway Northern Counties Committee (Ireland)**: 2-6-0 express passenger locomotive.

72 **Great Southern Railway (Eire)**: 3-cylinder 4-6-0 express locomotive *Maeve*.

73 **New Zealand Government Railways**: the Class 'Ab'
'Pacific' of 1915.

74 **New Zealand Government Railways**: the 'Wab'
class 4-6-4 tank engine of 1917.

75 **New Zealand Government Railways**: the 'K' class
4-8-4 of 1932.

76 **New Zealand Government Railways**: the 'J' class
streamlined 4-8-4.

MAXIMUM POWER ARTICULATEDS

EAST AFRICA

77 **Kenya and Uganda Railway**: the giant 'EC3' class
4-8-4+4-8-4 Beyer Garratt locomotive.

U.S.A.

78 **Denver and Rio Grande Western**: the 4-6-6-4 simple
articulated freight locomotive.

ENGLAND

79 **Southern Railway (England)**: the 'Schools' class 3-cylinder 4-4-0.

EGYPT

80 **Eygyptian State Railways**: 4-4-0 express passenger locomotive.

81 **Northern Railway of France**: 4-4-2 de Glehn
compound with Lemaitre front-end.

82 **Great Northern Railway of Ireland**: modernised
4-4-0 simple locomotive.

83　**Indian Broad Gauge Standard**: the 'XB' 'Pacific' class.

84　**Bengal Nagpur Railway**: the 'GSM' class 4–6–0 mail engine.

85 **North Western Railway (India):** Class 'XS2' 4-cylinder 'Pacific' express locomotive.

86 **Bengal Nagpur Railway:** 4-cylinder de Glehn compound 'Pacific'.

ENGLAND

87 **London and North Eastern Railway**: Thirsk new
signal box.

ENGLAND

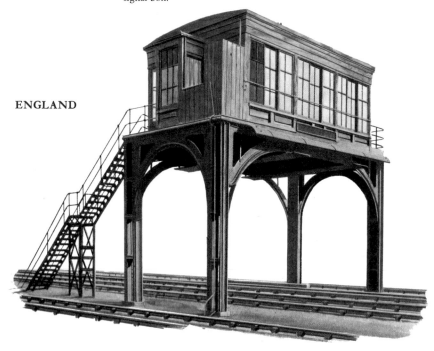

88 **Newcastle Central**: old signal box.

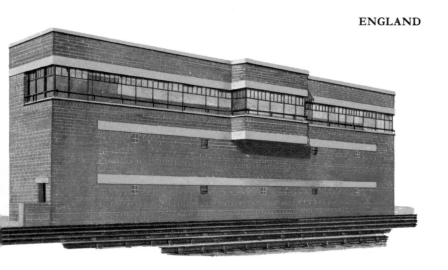

89 **Great Western Railway**: Bristol Temple Meads East, power signal box.

90 **Alsace-Lorraine Railways**: Mulhouse signal box.

MALAYA

91 **Malayan Railways**: 3-cylinder 'Pacific' express
passenger locomotive.

THAILAND

92 **Royal State Railways of Thailand**: American-built
3-cylinder 'Pacific' locomotive.

93   **Malayan Railways**: 2-cylinder 4-6-4 tank engine.

94   **Burma Railways**: 2-6-4 suburban tank locomotive.

95 **London, Midland and Scottish Railway**: the Stanier 'Black Five' mixed traffic 4-6-0.

96 **London, Midland and Scottish Railway**: the '5XP' 'Jubilee' class 4-6-0.

LARGE CONTINENTAL DESIGNS

FRANCE

97 **Paris, Lyons and Mediterranean Railway**: 4-cylinder compound 'Pacific'.

HOLLAND

98 **Netherlands State Railways**: 4-8-4 tank engine.

99 **South Australian Railways**: the '520' class lightweight
4–8–4.

100 **Victorian Railways**: Class 'X' 2–8–2 goods locomotive.

101 **Victorian Railways**: Class 'S' 4-6-2 express passenger
locomotive.

102 **Western Australian Government Railways**: 'Pacific'
type express goods locomotive Class 'PR'.

ENGLAND

103 **Great Western Railway**: the pioneer diesel mechanical railcar.

TURKEY

104 **Turkish State Railways**: steam railcar.

105 **London and North Eastern Railway**: 'Clayton' type
steam railcar.

106 **German Federal Railways**: the 'Glass' car working
tours from Munich.

107 **Atchison, Topeka & Sante Fé Railroad**: the '3771' class 4-8-4.

108 **Union Pacific Railroad**: 3-cylinder 4-12-2 heavy freight engine.

109 **London and North Eastern Railway**: the 'Royal Train' 4-4-0 (London-Wolferton).

110 **London, Midland and Scottish Railway**: the record-breaking Stanier 'Pacific' *Princess Elizabeth*.

111 **South African Railways**: the '15CA' 4-8-2 mixed traffic locomotive.

CHINA

112 **Chinese National Railways**: Canton–Hankow line. 4-8-4 mixed traffic locomotive of 1934.

CONTINENTAL VARIETIES

U.S.S.R.

113 **Soviet Russian Railways**: the standard 'Su' class 2-6-2 of 1932, 5ft. gauge.

ITALY

114 **Italian State Railways**: 4-cylinder 2-6-2 express locomotive.

115 **Madrid, Zaragoza and Alicante Railway**: mixed
traffic 4-8-0 locomotive.

116 **Finnish State Railways**: 2-8-2 Class Tr1 freight
locomotive.

MODERN COACH EVOLUTION

U.S.A.

117 **New York, New Haven and Hartford**: dining car for the 'Yankee Clipper' service.

AUSTRALIA

118 **Western Australian Government Railways**: Sleeping car for the 'Westland' express.

119 **Chicago, Milwaukee, St. Paul & Pacific Railroad**: Super-dome car.

120 **French National Railways**: third class corridor carriage.

SOUTH AMERICAN TYPES

B.A.G.S

121 **Buenos Aires Great Southern Railway**: Class '11c'
4-8-0 heavy goods engine (oil fired).

CENTRAL ARGENTINE

122 **Buenos Aires Great Southern Railway**: the '12G'
class 3-cylinder 'Pacific'.

123 **Buenos Aires Pacific Railway**: 2-8-2 mixed traffic locomotive.

124 **Buenos Aires Great Southern Railway**: the '12H' class 4-6-0.

ENGLAND

125 **London, Midland and Scottish Railway**: 20-ton
hopper wagon.

126 **Great Western Railway**: 10-ton fish van 'Bloater'.

127 **Belgian National Railways**: refrigerator van for international traffic.

128 **German State Railways**: all-welded 20-ton freight wagon.

129 **Canadian Pacific Railway**: the 'Royal Hudson' class
4–6–4.

130 **Canadian Pacific Railway**: 2–10–0 bank engine for
service in the Rocky Mountains.

131 **Canadian National Railways**: 4-6-4 express locomotive.

132 **Canadian Pacific Railway**: the '2800' 'Hudson' class
4-6-4.

EUROPEAN EIGHT-COUPLEDS

NORWAY

133 **Norwegian State Railways**: the 'Dovregubben' 2–8–4
type express passenger locomotive.

U.S.S.R.

134 **Soviet Russian Railways**: the 'IS' class 2–8–4 express
passenger locomotive of 1932.

135 **South Indian Railway**: Indian broad gauge standard
2-8-2 freight engine.

136 **Canadian Pacific Railway**: the 2-10-4 heavy passenger
locomotive for Rocky Mountain service.

137 **London and North Eastern Railway**: triplet articulated dining car set.

FRANCE

138 **International Sleeping Car Company**: Pullman car for the 'Golden Arrow' service in France.

139 **New Zealand Government Railways**: second-class
main line coach.

SUB-STANDARD GAUGE TYPES

U.S.A.

140 **Denver and Rio Grande Western**: narrow gauge
2–8–2 locomotive of Class K-36.

NIGERIA

141 **Nigerian Railways**: 4–8–0 type mixed traffic locomotive.

142 **South African Railways**: the Class '16c' 'Pacific'
express locomotive of 1919.

143 **Mysore State Railway**: metre-gauge 'Pacific' locomotive.

144 **Baltimore and Ohio Railroad**: an anglicised 'Pacific' locomotive of 1928.

145 **Baltimore and Ohio Railroad**: lightweight high speed 4-4-4 locomotive of 1934.

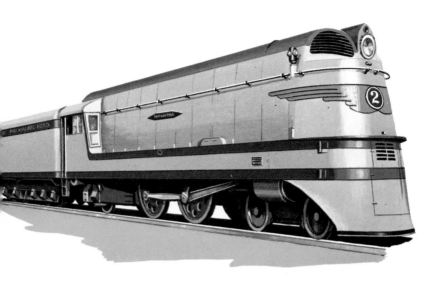

146 **Chicago, Milwaukee, St. Paul & Pacific Railroad**: streamlined 4-4-2 locomotive for the 'Hiawatha' express.

147 **New York Central Lines**: streamlined 4-6-4 locomotive for the 'Twentieth Century Limited'.

148 **Great Western Railway**: 'Castle' class 4-6-0 partially streamlined.

149 **London and North Eastern Railway**: streamlined 'Sandringham' class 4-6-0.

150 **London, Midland and Scottish Railway**: 'Coronation' streamlined 'Pacific' with casing opened to give access to smokebox.

HEAVY FREIGHT LOCOMOTIVES

ENGLAND

151 **London and North Eastern Railway**: the 'P1' class 2–8–2 heavy mineral engine.

FRANCE

152 **Northern Railway of France**: 2–10–0 compound freight engine.

153   **Great Northern Railway of U.S.A.**: Class 'R2'
2–8–8–2 of 1929.

154   **German State Railways**: Class '50' 2–10–0 heavy
freight locomotive.

EGYPT

155 **Egyptian State Railways**: 4-6-0 express passenger
locomotive.

EAST AFRICA

156 **Kenya and Uganda Railway**: 2-8-2 mail train engine.

157 **Indian Government Railway**: the 'XA' class standard broad gauge light Pacific.

158 **Gold Coast Railways**: 4-6-2 passenger and mail locomotive.

U.S.A.

159 **Norfolk and Western Railway**: the Class 'J' 4-8-4 express passenger locomotive.

ARGENTINE

160 **Buenos Aires Great Southern Railway**: the '12K' 2-cylinder 'Pacific' of 1939.

161 **South African Railways**: the '15F' class 4-8-2 mixed traffic locomotive.

162 **Rhodesia Railways**: the 15th class 4-6-4+4-6-4 fast passenger and mail 'Garratt'.

NOTABLE TANK ENGINE DESIGNS

FRANCE

163 **Northern Railway of France**: 2-8-2 suburban passenger tank engine.

ARGENTINE

164 **Buenos Aires Pacific Railway**: 4-6-4 suburban passenger tank engine.

ENGLAND

165 **Southern Railway (England)**: 2-6-4 fast passenger tank engine.

ARGENTINE

166 **Buenos Aires Great Southern Railway**: the Class '8E' 3-cylinder 2-6-4 tank engine.

SIGNAL GANTRIES AND BRACKETS

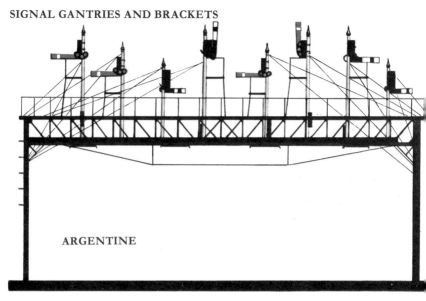

ARGENTINE

167 **Buenos Aires Great Southern Railway**: gantry of upper quadrant signals.

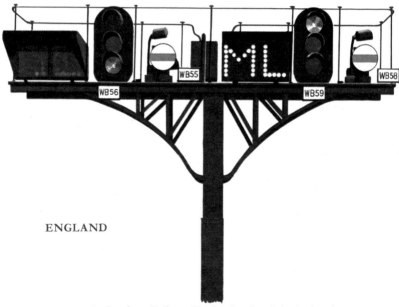

ENGLAND

168 **Southern Railway (England)**: colour light signals and route indicators at Waterloo.

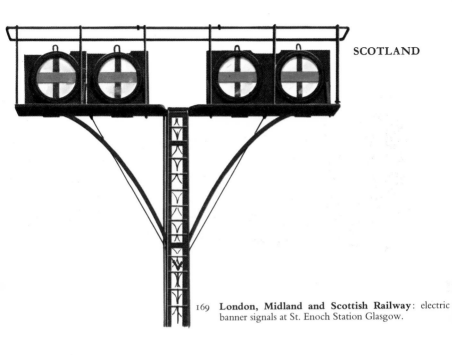

SCOTLAND

169 **London, Midland and Scottish Railway**: electric banner signals at St. Enoch Station Glasgow.

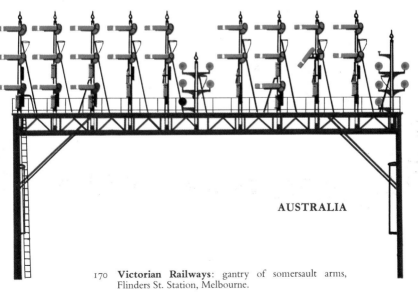

AUSTRALIA

170 **Victorian Railways**: gantry of somersault arms, Flinders St. Station, Melbourne.

NOTABLE CARRIAGES

BELGIUM

171   **Belgian National Railways**: first and second class
composite carriage for international service.

CANADA

172   **Canadian National Railways**: air-conditioned coach.

DENMARK

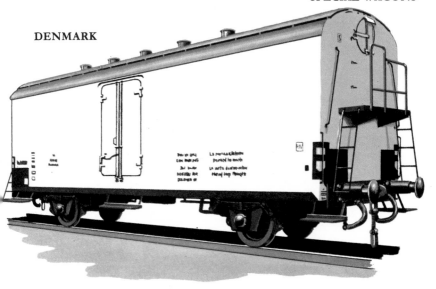

173 **Danish State Railways**: all-steel refrigerator van.

IRAQ

174 **Iraqi State Railways**: double–decked sheep van.

GOLD COAST

175 **Gold Coast Railways**: the '221' class heavy freight and mineral 4–8–2 locomotive.

ITALY

176 **Italian State Railways**: 2–6–0 passenger locomotive.

177 **Belgian National Railways**: semi-streamlined 'Pacific' locomotive.

178 **Hungarian State Railways**: 4-8-0 passenger loco-motive.

ENGLAND

179 **London and North Eastern Railway**: the Class 'A4'
'Pacific' *Dwight D. Eisenhower*.

GREAT BRITAIN

180 **London, Midland and Scottish Railway**: the
'Duchess' class 'Pacific' of 1938.

181 **Paris-Orleans-Midi Railway:** the Chapelon 4-8-0
(rebuilt from 4-6-2).

182 **New York Central Lines**: the 'Niagara' 4-8-4 high
speed locomotive.

GREAT BRITAIN

183 **London, Midland and Scottish Railway**: the Stanier 'Turbomotive'.

U.S.A.

184 **Great Northern Railway of U.S.A.**: a 4000 horse-power diesel–electric express locomotive.

RAILWAYS AT THE ZENITH OF STEAM
1920–40

1 Great Western Railway: The 'King George V' in the U.S.A.

In the year 1927 the Baltimore and Ohio Railroad celebrated its centenary, and among the great assembly of locomotives and relics that its management wished to display on that occasion a desire was expressed for an English locomotive. This project was put to Sir Felix Pole, General Manager to the Great Western Railway, and design and construction of the new super-'Castle' class 4–6–0, then in hand at Swindon Works, was speeded up in order that the first engine of the class should be ready for shipment to the U.S.A. in August 1927, in time to take part in the Centenary celebrations of the Baltimore and Ohio Railroad. This latest, most powerful, and most advanced of any British locomotive designs of the day created a tremendous impression in America, by the fine workmanship and finish, the handsome appearance, and the comparatively easy way it performed, with an almost complete absence of black smoke. Our picture shows the engine *King George V* as it appeared in the exhibition, with the lady portraying 'Britannia' on the running plate. At home the 'King' class engines, 30 in number, performed prodigies of hard running on the West of England and Wolverhampton services, and although introduced in 1927–30, they lasted out steam, and were withdrawn from the principal express-train services only when general dieselization took place from 1958 onwards. The 'Kings' were a very much larger and more powerful edition of the famous 'Castle' class, and had four cylinders $16\frac{1}{4}$ in. diameter by 28 in. stroke; 6 ft. 6 in. coupled wheels; a boiler pressure of 250 lb. per sq. in., and the weight of engine and tender in working order was $135\frac{3}{4}$ tons. The tractive effort was 40,300 lb.

2 Northern Railway of France: The 'Collin' Super-Pacific.

Just as the 'King' class 4–6–0 of the Great Western represented the ultimate development of all that has been finest in British practice in the pre-grouping era, so in France the Collin 'Pacifics' of the Nord can be considered as the ultimate expression of the famous De Glehn four-cylinder compounds, before the researches of Monsieur Chapelon on the Paris–Orléans–Midi Railway began to revolutionize design not only in France but in England as well. The Collin 'Pacifics' were splendid engines, first introduced in 1931. They had the characteristic, very short Nord boiler, with a deep firebox, that steamed very freely on poor-quality coal mixed with briquettes. These engines, which weighed 100 tons without their tenders, were designed to haul loads up to 650 tons at the maximum legal speed of $74\frac{1}{2}$ m.p.h. on level track and to mount the long gradients of 1 in 200 without the speed falling below 56 m.p.h. They worked the very heavy English boat trains between Paris and Calais at average speeds of 60 m.p.h., and ran the non-stop expresses then operating between Paris and Brussels, and between Paris and Liège. On these jobs the French drivers traversed considerable mileages of the Belgian National Railways. They were beautiful engines to ride, travelling always with the quiet and smoothness of a sewing machine; but because of the dusty, poor coal one always finished up as black as a sweep!

3 German State Railways : A Standard 'Pacific' Locomotive.

Prior to the unification of the railways of Germany a remarkably advanced locomotive practice had been developed in Bavaria, by co-operation between the railway authorities and the firm of Krauss-Maffei, of Munich. The development was of sufficient interest and importance to attract the attention of the English London and North Western Railway, and the famous Crewe-designed 'Claughton' class of 4–6–0 had one important feature that was derived directly from Bavaria. Maffei advanced from this 4–6–0 to the 'Pacific' type, and some excellent engines were produced—all four-cylinder compounds. Our picture shows a later version of this general design after it had been adopted as a national standard. An external feature that will be noted is the rather long chimney, in relation to other boiler mountings. The high-pressure cylinders, inside, are $17\frac{3}{8}$ in. dia. by 24 in. stroke, and the low-pressure $25\frac{5}{8}$ in. dia. by $26\frac{3}{8}$ in. stroke. Coupled wheels are 6 ft. $1\frac{5}{8}$ in. diameter, and boiler pressure 235 lb. per sq. in. The boiler is a large one, with 2168 sq. ft. of evaporative heating surface, 821 sq. ft. of superheating surface, and a grate area of $48\cdot4$ sq. ft. The engine alone weighs $95\frac{1}{4}$ tons.

4 Belgian National Railways : A Flamme 'Pacific'.

Among locomotives otherwise orthodox in their design these were some of the most unusual in appearance ever to take the road. They dated originally from 1909, but as shown in our picture, they were considerably rebuilt for the part they played in working the heavy express traffic between the two wars. Considered on basic dimensions they were an ordinary, if very large and powerful, four-cylinder 'Pacific'. They had a tractive force far in advance of any British locomotive of the 1909 period, 33,550 lb.; but the extraordinary feature of their design was the very short boiler, with the front of the smoke box so far back as to be in line with the rearmost bogie wheels, and all the 'engine' machinery out in front. Although the wheelbase was normal for a 'Pacific', the boiler, although so short, had a high evaporative capacity. The evaporative heating surface was 2570 sq. ft. and the superheating surface 692 sq. ft. The grate area was no less than $53\cdot8$ sq. ft. Our picture shows the engine as rebuilt with double-chimney, and fitted with the continental type of deflectors. There were two sets of safety valves mounted abreast of each other immediately behind the dome. Between the two wars these engines were much in demand for the heavy International express trains working south from Brussels over the heavy gradients of the Luxembourg line. Although looking so ungainly, they were good engines in traffic, and the majority had a life of more than forty years, through their various rebuildings.

5 Great Indian Peninsular Railway: 4–6–0 Express Passenger Locomotive of 1922.

In the first two decades of the twentieth century there was considerable difference of opinion among Indian locomotive engineers as to whether to make the 'Atlantic' or the 4–6–0 a standard. Some railways, such as the East Indian, used both or a considerable time. Gradually opinion set in favour of the 4–6–0, and the engine shown in our picture shows an advanced design for the immediate post-war period in which large-diameter piston valves, Walschaerts valve gear, and top feed take away some of the characteristic cleanness of line which Indian locomotives shared with their British counterparts in the 1900–14 period. This G.I.P.R. locomotive had cylinders 20½ in. diameter by 26 in. stroke; 6 ft. 2 in. coupled wheels, and worked at a pressure of 180 lb. per sq. in. Several of the Indian railways used 4–6–0s of general similar design, and it was from a synthesis of the best features of these that the Indian Railway locomotive Standards Committee, set up in 1924, evolved their first standard design, the 'H.P.S.' class 4–6–0, of which large numbers were ordered from Great Britain in the mid 1920s. The basic dimensions of the 'H.P.S.' were the same as those of the G.I.P. 4–6–0 illustrated.

6 Chicago and North Western Railway: Class 'E' 'Pacific' Locomotive of 1921.

In an earlier book of this series, dealing with locomotives at the turn of the century, reference was made to the part played by the Chicago and North Western Railway in establishing through communication between Chicago and the Pacific coast, in association with the Union Pacific and the Southern Pacific Railroads. The 4–4–0 locomotives introduced for working the celebrated 'Fast Mail' night service between Chicago and Omaha, and their successors of the 'Atlantic' type, were illustrated and described. Our present subject carries the story of C. & N.W.R. motive power a stage further to what may be termed the final phases of the moderate-sized American passenger locomotive. The

Class 'E' Pacific, introduced in 1921, would have been reckoned a very large and powerful engine by contemporary British standards, having two cylinders 25 in. diameter by 28 in. stroke; 6 ft. 3 in. coupled wheels; and a boiler with an evaporative heating surface of 3200 sq. ft., a super-heating surface of 778 sq. ft. and a grate area of 52·7 sq. ft. The boiler pressure was 185 lb. per sq. in. and the tractive effort 36,700 lb. Nevertheless, in a matter of two years these engines had been surpassed by the 'E2' class, with tractive effort increased to 45,000 lb., and in 1929 the C. & N.W.R. 'went big' with a vengeance, introducing the 'H' class 4–8–4, with a tractive effort of 71,800 lb. and a total weight of engine and tender, in working order, of 365 tons! Despite such spectacular development, however, the 'E' class engines of 1921 filled a most important role in the development of railway motive power in the U.S.A.

7 Swiss Federal Railways: A Four-cylinder Compound 4–6–0 for the Gotthard Line.

Prior to its electrification, the Gotthard Line was one of the most difficult railways to operate in all Europe. Between Erstfeld, on the northern side of the great tunnel, and Bellinzona the line climbs for many miles at the extremely steep inclination of 1 in 37, and even to achieve a gradient no worse than this there are several spiral locations where the track is carried deep into the mountainsides. On passing through the Gotthard tunnel and reaching the canton of Ticino there is an equally steep descent. At the turn of the century the line was worked by four-cylinder compound 4–6–0s of French design, but when more powerful locomotives were needed a contract was placed with the celebrated Bavarian firm of Maffei, of

Munich. The type of locomotive shown in our picture, a four-cylinder compound, with all four cylinders driving on to the leading pair of coupled wheels, saw steam out on the Gotthard line. They were designed to work at a maximum speed of 55 m.p.h. on the straighter and more level stretches of line and to climb the great inclines at about 25 m.p.h. with a train of about 200 tons. With the heavy International trains these engines often worked in pairs.

8 **Swedish State Railways:** The Class 'F' Express Passenger 'Pacific'.

These handsome engines, originally introduced in 1914, were the largest and most powerful passenger type to be built for service in Sweden. They were four-cylinder compounds with the high-pressure cylinders inside, and the large low-pressure cylinders outside and somewhat steeply inclined. It may seem a little strange that the ultimate development of steam power for express passenger trains in Sweden should have been made as long ago as 1914; but Sweden was early in the field for railway electrification, and these engines, originally used on the Stockholm–Malmo trains were later moved to the Laxa–Charlottenberg route, after the electrification of the former. On the Charlottenberg line they worked on the Stockholm–Oslo expresses, until that line was also electrified. After that they were sold to the Danish State Railways, where they continued to do good work for many years. Their principal dimensions were: cylinders, high-pressure, $16\frac{1}{2}$ in. diameter, low-pressure $24\frac{3}{4}$ in. diameter, with a common stroke of 26 in.; the coupled wheels were 6 ft. 2 in. diameter, and the total weight of engine and tender in working order $140\frac{1}{2}$ tons.

9 **Southern Railway (England):** The 'King Arthur' Class 4-6-0.

In Great Britain from the turn of the century the tendency in locomotives of maximum power for express passenger work was to use various multi-cylindered systems of propulsion: three or four cylinders, sometimes with single-expansion and sometimes with compound propulsion. This trait was nowhere more marked than on the London and South Western Railway, under Dugald Drummond. When R. W. Urie succeeded to the office of Chief Mechanical Engineer, after Drummond's death in 1912, a complete change in policy took place, and one that was at variance with contemporary practice in Great Britain. Urie used two cylinders only, with all the motion work outside. In this he set a pattern that became almost universal in America, and was eventually adopted on the range of standard locomotives built by the nationalized railways from 1951 onwards. The 'King Arthur' class of 1925 was a development of Urie's 'N15' 4-6-0 of 1918 wholly in the two-cylinder tradition, but incorporating by R. E. L. Maunsell certain refinements in valve gear and draughting design that made them really great engines. The 'King Arthurs' were very simple and straightforward, capable of heavy pulling and high speed. The engine illustrated, No. 784, *Sir Nerovens*, was one of a batch of thirty built by the North British Locomotive Co. Ltd., and for that reason known on the Southern Railway as the 'Scotch Arthurs'. The entire class was named after knights of the Round Table, and other personalities associated with the legend of King Arthur. The dimensions of the locomotives were: cylinders (two) $20\frac{1}{2}$ in. diameter by 28 in. stroke; coupled wheels 6 ft. 7 in. diameter; heating surfaces, evaporative 1878 sq. ft., superheater 337 sq. ft., grate area 30 sq. ft.; boiler pressure 200 lb. per sq. in., tractive effort 25,320 lb.

10 **Austrian State Railways:** 4–8–0 General Service Locomotive.

The 4–8–0 proved a popular type in Austria, Hungary, and Spain, where the wheel arrangement was particularly suitable to heavy working on mountain grades. The objection to it in some countries was that the presence of driving wheels at the rear end limited the size of the firebox; and this was an important consideration in countries where poor coal made desirable the largest possible grate. But in Austria, particularly, the height of the loading gauge made it possible to pitch the boiler unusually high, and on these 4–8–0s, introduced in 1923, the grate area was 47 sq. ft. They were singularly angular and unaesthetic locomotives, though they have put in many years of excellent work on the line, especially in taking heavy International trains over the Semmering Pass. Unlike most Austrian locomotives of the preceding years, they were not compounds. The two cylinders were 22 in. diameter by 28·35 in. stroke; coupled-wheel diameter was 5 ft. 2 in., and the large boiler had an evaporative heating surface of 2345 sq. ft. and a super-heating surface of 641 sq. ft. Boiler pressure was 213 lb. per sq. in. and the tractive effort 34,066 sq. ft. They may not have been handsome engines, but they certainly proved worth extensive modernisation in the early 1950s, when they were fitted with the Giesl ejector.

11 **Great Western Railway:** 70-ft. Bogie Corridor Carriage of 1923.

In the early 1900s the Great Western Railway introduced very long carriages in order to convey the maximum number of passengers for the minimum dead weight of rolling stock. Journeys on the Inter-City business trains and on the holiday expresses from London to South Devon did not call for the same degree of luxury as on expresses running, for example, from London to Scotland. The earlier examples of such coaches were built in the traditional style with timber-panelled bodies on steel frames; but when the time came for the new stock to be introduced, after the First World War the bodies were constructed with smooth-sided steel panelling, thus introducing a degree of streamlining. Our picture shows a 10-compartment third-class carriage, providing seats for 80 passengers. Because of the inclusion of certain amenities, the tare weight of the new coaches was greater than the pre-war examples, but even so, a tare weight of 37 tons for a seating capacity of 80 is low, by modern standards. These new coaches, although divested of the old form of panelling, were elaborately lined out on the flat sheeting, and at a first glance had the appearance of recessed panel work. In later years, as an economy measure, the elaborate lining out was abandoned, and only the change from cream to chocolate at the waistline marked by a very simple lining out in gold.

12 **Italian State Railways:** Corridor Carriage.

In the 1930s, when efforts were being made in all parts of the world to improve railway efficiency, many attempts were made to reduce the dead weight to be hauled by locomotives. The use of articulated coaches by the London and North Eastern Railway is noticed elsewhere in this volume. The Italian State Railways succeeded in reducing the dead weight per seat by introducing light metals into the construction of the coaches without impairing their rigidity. The coach illustrated is one of a series indicating the advance in constructional techniques between the years 1921 and 1932. In the former year the standard main-line corridor carriages had a tare weight of 42·1 tons. Depending upon the space provided for passengers, the seating was 42 in a first-class carriage of this weight, 64 in a 'second', and 80 in a third. By use of the light-weight techniques it was found possible to construct larger and more commodious carriages of exactly the same tare weight, but having a seating capacity of 48 'firsts', 72 'seconds', and 88 'thirds'—an increase of 10–15 per cent. The new coaches, as will be seen from our picture, are very long and handsome vehicles, having a length over buffers of 76 ft. and an overall width of 9 ft. 7 in.

13 **German State Railways:** Corridor Carriage.

At the same time as the Italian developments in light-weight coach design were taking place a parallel development was taking place in Germany, by the introduction of modern electric-welding techniques. It must be admitted that most continental railway coaches were much heavier than contemporary British designs, but the distances to be covered were longer, and the methods of construction, by tradition, more massive. German engineers attacked the problem of weight reduction by the extensive use of welding, in place of riveting. By avoidance of the double thicknesses at riveted joints, and the additional weight of the rivet heads, considerable reductions in weight of the bogies was effected, while the entire underframe and the body framing was

built up as a single integrated fabrication. The composite second- and third-class carriage shown in our picture is an example of welded construction, in which the dead weight was brought down from 47 to 34 tons. This reduction of more than 20 per cent meant that with a full train of these vehicles a locomotive could haul a longer train, with a greater pay-load, than previously, or that the same number of passengers could be hauled at the same speed for a reduced coal consumption, because of the lesser demand for power output.

14 **Rhodesia Railways:** First-class Sleeping Car.

From its nodal point at Bulawayo the Rhodesia Railways operate long-distance express-train services in three directions: to Salisbury, and thence to the Indian Ocean port of Beira; to the Victoria Falls, on the route originally planned as part of the 'Cape-to-Cairo' railway; and southwards to Johannesburg and Cape Town. On some of these runs a passenger can spend two or more nights in the train, and, as in South Africa, the stock is designed to be readily convertible from night to day use. The berths are usually changed from the day to the night position, or vice versa, while passengers are in the dining-car, either at breakfast or dinner. These beautiful cars, built by the Gloucester Railway Carriage and Wagon Company, have three single and four double compartments, providing sleeping accommodation for 22 passengers. When the berths are swung into their day position, and arranged as seats, there is accommodation for 33 to sit down. On a long journey the train inevitably assumes something of the air of a hotel, and it is pleasant to have additional seating in one's cabin where friends can 'drop in', as it were, in the course of the journey. An interesting feature of these cars, common enough in Africa, are the end-balcony entrances, where one can stand and get a wider view of the passing scene.

15 Great Southern Railway (Eire): 2-6-2 Tank Engine.

Following the grouping of the railways in Great Britain, in 1923, legislation was introduced for similar grouping in Ireland, and there all railways in Eire, with the exception of the Great Northern, were brought under one management named the Great Southern. The Great Northern was an international concern, and so could not be included also. In addition to the two major companies included in the G.S.R., namely the former Great Southern and Western, and the Midland Great Western, the new company included a number of smaller railways, and to provide a standard type of locomotive for working over such sections as the former Dublin and South Eastern, Cork, Bandon and South Coast, and other sections which had short-distance passenger traffic Mr J. R. Bazin, the Chief Mechanical Engineer, designed a smart little 2-6-2 tank, generally similar in its style to the 4-6-0 passenger engines, reference 72. The 2-6-2 tanks had two cylinders, $17\frac{1}{2}$ in. diameter by 28 in. stroke; coupled wheel diameter 5 ft. 6 in.; a boiler having 816 sq. ft. evaporative heating surface and 240 sq. ft. super-heating, and a grate area of $19\frac{3}{4}$ sq. ft. The total weight of this useful little engine was $71\frac{1}{2}$ tons.

16 Netherlands Railways: 4-6-4 Tank Engine.

The first batch of these splendid engines were built in England, by Beyer Peacock and Co. just before the First World War. Although specified by Mr S. E. Haagsma, the Dutch locomotive superintendent, the detailed design was typically British of the period, and characteristic of the manu-facturers, even to the extent of the makers' plate carried in the form of a 'nameplate' over the leading coupled-wheel splasher. The only feature that detracted from an exceptionally neat outline was the height of the chimney over the other boiler mountings. The concealment of all the running gear was typical of British rather than of Continental practice, especially as the valve gear was Walschaerts. The cylinders were 20 in. diameter by 26 in. stroke; coupled wheels 6 ft. 1 in. diameter; the total heating surface was 1710 sq. ft., and the working pressure 170 lb. per sq. in. The total weight of the engine in working order was 91 tons. A design feature that contributed to the free running and gener-ally economical performance of these engines was the large diameter of the piston valves in relation to the size of the cylinders, $9\frac{7}{8}$ in. diameter, permitting of a very free flow of steam into and out of the cylinders.

17 Czecho-Slovakian Railways: 2-8-4 Tank Engine.

The railways of Czecho-Slovakia include many sections of heavy grading, and on account of its geographical situation in Europe much of the main-line passenger traffic is of an international character. In 1931 the impressive and powerful class of 2-8-4 tank engine that we illustrate was introduced specially for the mountain sections. Unlike many contemporary locomotives on the continent of Europe, these engines were two-cylinder simples, built by the firm of Ceskomaravska-Kolben-Danek, of Prague. These engines were designed for a maximum speed of $46\frac{1}{2}$ m.p.h., and as strict observance of speed limits is essential on the difficult routes traversed, they were fitted with recording speedometers, making a continuous record of the speed throughout the run. The English equivalents of their basic dimensions were: cylinders 23·62 in. diameter by 28·35 in. stroke, coupled wheels 5 ft. 4 in. diameter, boiler, 2336 sq. ft. evaporative heating surface and 891·8 sq. ft. superheating surface, grate area 47·34 sq. ft. Total weight in working order $107\frac{1}{2}$ tons. Electric lighting, including the driver's cab, was fitted throughout. They were coal fired, though using the rather low-grade coal frequently found in central European countries.

18 Bengal Nagpur Railway: 2–8–2 Tank Engine.

The fourth of this group of tank engines is a powerful shunting and freight type, of characteristically British appearance, for local working on the Bengal Nagpur Railway. In short-distance working, and the kind of intermittent duty for which these locomotives were designed, it was not always advantageous to use superheated steam. A locomotive takes a little time, to use a colloquialism, 'to get its superheat', and the cost of providing the equipment with the associated need of special features of lubrication is not always worth the trouble. These engines, built in Glasgow by the North British Locomotive Company, had coupled wheels only 4 ft. 3 in. diameter; the cylinders were 20 in. diameter by 26 in. stroke with piston valves actuated by the Walschaerts gear. With a boiler pressure of 180 lb. per sq. in. this provided a powerful engine with a tractive force of 27,500 lb. The total weight in working order was 79 tons. The boiler had a total heating surface of 1450 sq. ft., and the grate area was $27\frac{1}{4}$ sq. ft. Although so British in appearance, with a chimney strongly reminiscent of Pickersgill engines on the Caledonian, the louvred shade on the cab side adds the true Indian flavour.

19 Austrian State Railways: 2–8–4 Express Locomotive.

It is certainly appropriate to begin this quartet of larger Continental express passenger locomotives with this very notable Austrian design. It was a natural development, from the wheel-arrangement point of view, from the celebrated 2–6–4 compounds of Karl Gölsdorf, but there the analogy ceased. The 2–8–4 of 1928 was a new design in every respect, not least in being a two-cylinder simple. Very powerful locomotives were needed to run the International expresses west of Vienna to accelerated timings on the section to Salzburg. No more than 13 were needed for the workings in Austria, but no fewer than 79 further examples of the design, identical in every respect, were put into service in Rumania. The cylinders were 25·6 in. diameter by 28·35 in. stroke; the coupled-wheel diameter was 6 ft. $4\frac{1}{2}$ in., and the boiler had 3000 sq. ft. of evaporative heating surface, 979 sq. ft. of superheating surface, and a grate area of 50·8 sq. ft. The tractive effort was 44,030 lb. They were designed for a maximum service speed of 75 m.p.h., but on test one of them was successfully run up to 96 m.p.h. More important, perhaps, was their ability to climb the heavy gradients at each end of the main line, westwards through the Vienna Woods, and eastwards from Salzburg.

20 Eastern Railway of France: 4–8–2 Compound Express Locomotive.

The Eastern Railway of France operated a very heavy traffic on two major routes eastward from Paris: to Strasbourg, *en route* for South Germany, and the route of the Orient Express to Vienna and the Balkans, and to Belfort, for Switzerland, and entry to Austria via the Arlberg route. Limitations in maximum axle load precluded any worthwhile enlargement of the existing 4–6–0 and 4–6–2 type locomotives, and so in 1930 the huge 4–8–2 shown in our picture was introduced by Monsieur Duchatel. Forty-two of these locomotives were put into service in 1930–31. As usual with the de Glehn system of compounding, the high-pressure cylinders were outside, driving the second pair of coupled wheels, and the low-pressure cylinders inside, and driving the leading pair. A very high boiler pressure, for that period, of 290 lb. per sq. in. was used, in a boiler having a total evaporative heating surface of 2401 sq. ft. and a superheating surface of 1013 sq. ft. The very large grate of 47½ sq. ft. was hand fired. The introduction of these large engines enabled trains of 550–700 tons to be worked satisfactorily, and the performance was demonstrated in some special trials between Paris and Cherbourg on the State railway system.

21 Paris, Lyons, and Mediterranean Railway: 4–8–2 Compound Express Locomotive.

The main line of this famous route from Paris to the South of France follows a very gradually rising course for the first 100 miles, and then the degree of ascent becomes more severe, culminating in a heavy climb on a gradient of 1 in 125 to the crest of the Cote d'Or mountains, at Blaisy Bas. While Pacific locomotives (ref. 97) could conveniently handle the heaviest trains over most of the line, something more powerful was needed for the mountain section between Laroche and Dijon, and in 1925 the magnificent 4–8–2 class illustrated was introduced. The low-pressure cylinders were outside and drove on to the leading pair of coupled wheels, while the high-pressure cylinders were inside, located behind the bogie and driving the second pair. As can be seen, the boiler was very large, with an evaporative heating surface of 2752 sq. ft. and a superheating surface of 1226 sq. ft. The grate area was 54 sq. ft. The engine alone weighed 115¼ tons in working order, and the tractive effort was 47,385 lb. The great size and elegant proportions of these engines was set off by the conical front to the smoke box. The engines were, however, designed for hill climbing rather than high speed, and the coupled wheels were no more than 5 ft. 10 in. diameter.

22 Spanish National Railway (R.E.N.F.E.): ex-Norte 4–8–2 Express Locomotive.

The Northern Railway was the first in Spain to use the 4–8–2 type. The main line from Madrid to the Biscay coast at Santander is very heavily graded, and the most difficult sections have now been electrified. But these giant compound 4–8–2s are still to be found in passenger service. Our picture shows one of them as rebuilt with double blast pipe and chimney. The sixty-five locomotives of this class were introduced at various times between 1925 and 1930, from various Spanish manufacturers including Maquinista, Euskalduna, and Babcock and

Wilcox of Bilbao. They are among the few Spanish locomotives on the national system to have a lined livery; the majority are plain black. Their leading dimensions are: cylinders, high pressure, $18\frac{1}{4}$ in. diameter; low pressure, $27\frac{1}{2}$ in. diameter, with a common stroke of $26\frac{3}{4}$ in. The coupled wheels are 5 ft. $8\frac{1}{2}$ in. diameter, and the total weight of engine and tender in working order is 161 tons. At the time of their introduction they were among the heaviest passenger engines in Europe.

23 **Pennsylvania Railroad:** The 'K4s' 'Pacific.'

This is probably one of the most famous locomotive designs ever to have been evolved in the U.S.A. The Pennsylvania itself was one of the greatest of American railroads, and its traffic in the period between the two world wars was enormous. The 'K4' was greatly eclipsed in size by the express passenger locomotives of many other lines, when wheel arrangements extended to the 4-6-4, 4-8-2, and 4-8-4 types; but the 'K4' Pacific remained a classic, and a great favourite on the line of its origin. In the later 1930s train speeds so increased, and train loads likewise, that on some of the heaviest duties it became necessary to work these great engines in pairs. The engine illustrated is one of a batch of 75 built in 1927 by the Baldwin Locomotive Works. Notable technical features of the design are the tapered boiler barrel; the unusual provision, on large American locomotives, of the Belpaire type of firebox; and the very simple, straightforward layout of the machinery, with only two cylinders. These latter are 27 in. diameter by 28 in. stroke; the coupled-wheel diameter is 6 ft. 8 in., and the enormous firebox has a grate area of 70 sq. ft. The evaporation heating surface is 4058 sq. ft. and the superheating surface 962 sq. ft. Boiler pressure, 205 lb. per sq. in. The total weight in working order of engine and tender is 237 tons, and yet the nominal tractive effort, of 44,460 lb., is not very much greater than that of an English Great Western 'King'.

24 **Baltimore and Ohio:** Class EL-5A 2-8-8-0 Simple Articulated Locomotive.

Like many railroads in the U.S.A., the Baltimore and Ohio adopted the Mallet articulated type in order to secure enhanced power for heavy freight working. In fact, the very first Mallet engine in the U.S.A. was built for this line in 1904. Success with this engine led to the purchase of no fewer than 133 engines of the 2-8-8-0 type during the years 1916-20. These were all true Mallets, in that they were compounds. But any economies in fuel consumption from the use of the compound principle were offset by high maintenance costs and sluggish running, and in the late 1920s George H. Emerson, the Chief of Motive Power, rebuilt one of them as a single-expansion engine with four cylinders 24 in. in diameter by 32 in. stroke, all taking live steam from the boiler. This made a remarkable improvement in all-round performance, and followed the trend that was then becoming marked in the U.S.A., namely to avoid the compound principle in all new locomotives of maximum power. These engines were coal burners, and had the high tractive effort of 118,800 lb. The heating surfaces were 5784 sq. ft. evaporative and 1415 sq. ft. superheating, while the grate area was $88\frac{1}{4}$ sq. ft. The weight of engine and tender in working order was 315 tons. In the Allegheny Mountain district these engines worked maximum-tonnage trains on gradients of 1 in 37½. Following the first experimental rebuilding, the whole stud was converted from compound to single-expansion working.

25 Atchison, Topeka, and Santa Fe Railroad: 2–10–4 Express Freight Engine.

The 'Santa Fé', to use the abbreviated name by which this celebrated railway is generally known, has a vastly greater extent than its name suggests. Its main line, indeed, stretches from Chicago, via Kansas City, through some of the wildest and most mountainous districts of Colorado and Arizona to the Pacific coast at Los Angeles. In the central districts the gradients are exceedingly severe, and the railroad began using ten-coupled locomotives for freight as early as the year 1902. The need for flexibility of wheelbase on the mountain divisions led to the development of the 2–10–2 type, in 1903, and as this was the first time it had been used, it was appropriately called the 'Santa Fé'. Between 1903 and 1926 large numbers of 2–10–2 locomotives were put on to the road, until the need for still larger fireboxes led to the introduction of the 2–10–4 type in 1930. Our picture illustrates the first of these enormous non-articulated engines. There are only two cylinders, but they are 30 in. diameter by 34 in. stroke; the coupled wheels are 5 ft. 9 in. diameter, and the boiler carries the very high pressure of 300 lb. per sq. in. The earliest examples of this type were coal fired, with mechanical stokers. This latter feature was very necessary with a grate having an area of 121 sq. ft. The total weight of engine and tender was no less than 393 tons, and the tractive effort 93,000 lb. Today the Santa Fé, like most American railways, has completely abolished steam, and the work once done by these engines is done by diesel–electric locomotives in tandem.

26 Lehigh and New England Railroad: An 0–8–0 'Switcher'.

It must be explained at once that the term 'switcher' is American railway parlance for a shunting locomotive, and the one chosen for illustration was built in 1927 for one of the smaller railways of the U.S.A. It served a rich industrial region somewhat apart from the main arteries of American railway business; but because of the great mineral deposits, it was an important 'feeder' line, connecting at various points and at its extremities with some of the largest railways in the U.S.A., including the Pennsylvania. Much of its traffic was in coal, and in dealing with the different requirements of customers and the different grades from the various coal-fields, much shunting was involved. In earlier days this relatively small railway made extensive use of the 'Mother Hubbard' type of locomotive, with cab mounted half-way along the boiler. This type was used for shunting duties—why, it is a little hard to understand, because the original idea of the 'Mother Hubbard' was to improve the driver's outlook on a fast run, when the look-out would be obscured by steam beating down. In the very large engine illustrated an orthodox layout is used. The tender is very large, to provide adequate fuel for long spells of duty without the need to return to shed for refuelling. The coupled wheels are placed very close together to enable the engine to negotiate sharp curves in marshalling yards. The tractive effort is high, 68,500 lb., to enable rapid acceleration of heavy loads to be made.

27 New South Wales Government Railways: The 'C36' Class Express Passenger 4–6–0.

This is one of the most celebrated express locomotive classes ever to work in Australia. It was first introduced in 1925, 10 being built at the railways' own Eveleigh works, and 65 by the Clyde Engineering Company. They were designed for long runs, both northbound and southbound from Sydney to the State boundaries, with express trains having non-stop runs up to 100 miles in their schedules; and to require the minimum of servicing so that they could return to their home depot without shed attention at the outer terminal points. They were extremely reliable in service, and worked all the principal expresses until the introduction of the 'C38' class in 1943. When more powerful locomotives were needed for the long run across the Nullarbor desert of the Commonwealth line, linking South with Western Australia it was a great compliment to the New South Wales railways that the 'C36' should have been chosen in 1937. In this duty they had a special high-capacity tender to carry them through a waterless country. They had two cylinders 23 in. diameter by 26 in. stroke; coupled wheels 5 ft. 9 in. diameter and a tractive effort of 30,500 lb. The total weight of engine and tender in working order was $159\frac{1}{4}$ tons.

28 New South Wales Government Railways: The 'D57' Heavy Goods 4–8–2.

These large freight engines, which with their tenders weighed 223 tons, were introduced in 1929 for the heaviest duties radiating from Sydney. They were of particular interest at the time, because to secure an even torque when starting maximum-load trains they were designed with three cylinders. Furthermore, they were fitted with the Gresley conjugated valve motion for the inside cylinder. Having regard to the enormous girth of the boiler, and the difficulty of getting access to any machinery inside, the Gresley gear provided an admirable solution. The combination levers, by which the motion for the inside cylinder valves was derived from the outside gears, can be seen in our picture, just above the buffer beam. With a tractive effort of 56,000 lb., these engines were the most powerful non-articulated class of steam locomotives in Australia. There were 25 of them in all, built in 1929 and 1930. Their three cylinders were $23\frac{1}{4}$ in. diameter by 28 in. stroke, coupled wheels 5 ft. diameter, and boiler pressure 200 lb. per sq. in. Owing to their great weight, their sphere of activity was limited: to Thirroul on the Illawarra line; to Junee on the Southern main line; and to Wallerawang on the Western line.

29 New South Wales Government Railways: The 'C32' Class 4–6–0 Express Passenger Engine.

The 'C32' class, to use the later and present designation, provided the backbone of the passenger working in New South Wales, for upwards of thirty years. As the celebrated 'P' class it originated as long ago as 1891, the first examples being built by Beyer, Peacock, and Company. But the design proved so successful that many more were added to the stock, some built in the U.S.A., others in Australia, but the greater number still in England, by Beyer, Peacock. Over the years many improvements were made to the actual engines in service. They were fitted with super-heaters and extended smokeboxes. The standard colour was black, but in the 1930s, when certain special new express trains were introduced, a number of the 'C32' class engines were selected for particular duties, and painting in styles other than black commenced. In 1933 two of them were painted a pastoral green, for express service on the Illawarra line, while in the same year four others were painted maroon, and named, for working the Sydney–Newcastle expresses. The engine in our picture, No. 3265 *Hunter*, was originally built in 1902, by Beyer, Peacock, and had thus done more than thirty years of service before her selection for special duties, and special painting.

30 New South Wales Government Railways: The 'C35' Class 4–6–0.

Until the introduction of the 'C38' class Pacific in 1943, the New South Wales Government Railways had relied entirely upon the 4–6–0 type for express passenger traffic, and the 'C35' formed an interesting stage in the gradual process of enlargement from the classic 'C32' of 1892, featured in an earlier volume in this series to the 'C36' (ref. 27). In the first decade of this century the Australian railways were feeling the effects of increased amenities in passenger travel. Heavy corridor coaches, dining and sleeping cars had been introduced on the principal expresses, and in New South Wales there was much double heading. The 'C35' was a pre-war design, to overcome this disadvantage, but its sphere of activity extended throughout the period of this book. The 35 engines of the class were built at various dates between 1914 and 1923. They belonged to the period of neat external appearance, inside valve gears, and

a typically British set of boiler mountings. The cabs were, however, closed in at a later date. Displaced over the years by the more powerful 'C36', they finally did much useful work on the northern line between Newcastle and South Brisbane. Although their tractive effort of 25,400 lb. was not greatly less than that of the 'C36', the boilers were considerably smaller.

31 London, Midland and Scottish Railway: Twelve-wheeled Dining and Kitchen Car.

The L.M.S.R., as successor to the London and North Western and Midland Railways, was always in the very front rank of carriage-building practice. For a few years after the grouping a number of important express trains were equipped with three-coach dining sets, consisting of first- and third-class saloons and a kitchen car between. These sets had a tare weight of about 90 tons, but it was found that the amount of accommodation needed for first-class dining was not so large as third class, and it became the practice to build the kitchen and the first-class saloon into a single 12-wheeled vehicle of about 45 tons tare weight, thus saving about 15 tons dead weight for each dining set. These combined dining and kitchen cars were most beautiful vehicles in which to ride. They had steel underframes, but the body framing was of teak, with the sides, ends, and roof steel panelled. That teak framing made a wonderful difference to the 'feel' of the car. It gave a quiet solidarity which was absent in the all-steel cars coming into service on the Continent. In the latter one was always conscious of the steel doors, and the way they clanged when shut. The L.M.S.R. cars were among the finest to run anywhere prior to 1940.

32 Southern Railway (England): Pullman Car.

The London Brighton and South Coast, and the South Eastern and Chatham Railways, both constituents of the Southern Railway formed by the grouping of 1923, were extensive users of Pullman cars. On their relatively short-distance runs neither company used corridor carriages, but for patrons who required extra comfort and the convenience of a buffet service, Pullman cars were included in many of the more important trains. The all-Pullman 'Southern Belle', running non-stop between London and Brighton, was one of the most popular trains in the country. After grouping the idea of luxury all-Pullman trains was extended to the former London and South Western line, and the car illustrated in our picture was one built specially for the 'Bournemouth Belle' service. Earlier Pullman cars were built in the traditional style with timber framing and panelling; but these new cars introduced in 1931 were of all-steel construction. Although having flush-sided bodies, they retained the characteristic Pullman appearance, with vestibuled ends, and the handsome chocolate and cream livery. The first-class cars were named, using single feminine Christian names, but the third class were only numbered. These cars were built by the Birmingham Railway Carriage & Wagon Company.

33 Atchison, Topeka, and Santa Fé: Dining Car of Trans-continental Expresses.

At the beginning of the period under review the typical American carriage on long-distance express trains had a high, clerestory-shaped roof, a very plain exterior finish, and was of very massive construction. The Santa Fé dining-car in our picture fully conformed to this general conception. They were of all-steel construction, were 80 ft. long over the end sills, and weighed 75 tons. In this they make an interesting comparison with the English car of the London Midland and Scottish Railway (ref. 31). Both had the kitchens incorporated, and the American car had a seating capacity of 36, at six single tables and six doubles, whereas the English car seated 24 first-class passengers. The latter were most sumptuously upholstered armchair settees, whereas the Santa Fé dining-car had loose upright chairs. The American cars had some very long journeys to make, throughout from Chicago to Los Angeles, and no doubt would have served several sittings at each meal. In the English cars one could often travel the entire journey in the luxury of the dining-car. On the American cars the kitchen and pantry arrangements were very comprehensive, to provide for the many meals required on the long journey.

34 Sudan Government Railways: Third-class Carriage.

The conditions of railway travel in hot, dry countries have always received special consideration from the manufacturers of rolling stock, in consultation with the users, and the new coaches built for the Sudan in 1930 by the Gloucester Railway Carriage and Wagon Company provide a fine example of the style of the period, utilising a steel-bodied construction. These coaches, finished externally in the 'cream velour' style standard on the Sudan Government Railways, have the old-fashioned sun shades extending the full length of the cars over the windows. Internally the seating is of the open saloon type, divided into two compartments only, with lavatories in the centre. Although of steel construction, the interiors had pitch-pine framing with steel panels painted stone colour. As would be expected, the seating arrangements for third-class passengers are quite simple. The seats are of the fixed type constructed of pitch-pine laths and varnished. The rail gauge is 3 ft. 6 in., but the loading gauge is liberal, permitting of an overall width of nearly 10 ft., and seating 56 passengers in comfort. The tare weight of these coaches was no more than 26¾ tons, a result achieved by skilful use of steel construction in design.

35 Rhodesia Railways: 4-8-2 Passenger and Mail Engine.

From its headquarters at Bulawayo the Rhodesia Railways operates three long and difficult main lines; difficult in that they pass through a high, sparsely populated country with long distances between stations, and single-line working, and also that the majority of the trains are very heavy. No high speeds are called for, and the runs include much hard pulling on severely curved and graded stretches of line. As in the Cape of Good Hope, the 4-8-0 type of locomotive was used from an early date, but the need for a locomotive with a larger firebox led to the introduction of the 4-8-2 type, and the so-called '12th class', which is the subject of our picture, has proved one of the most popular and successful designs ever to run in Southern Africa. Although very large articulated locomotives of the Beyer-Garratt type have been extensively used in Rhodesia for many years, the 12th class has remained the 'maid of all work', and until quite recently hauled most of the trains on the line from Bulawayo to the south via the state of Bechuanaland (now Botswana).

36 South African Railways: The 'MJ' Class Mallet Articulated 2-6-6-0 Compound.

The heavy gradients and severe curvature on some of the principal routes of the South African Railways led to the use of powerful articulated locomotives, and some interesting examples of the Mallet type were built by the North British Locomotive Co. Ltd. The 'MJ' class was used for rear-end banking on the heavy ascent of the Hex River pass, in Cape Province, between De Doorns and Matroosburg. In this distance of 16 miles the average inclination is 1 in 53, and on the most severe section it is 1 in 43 for 5 miles. These powerful engines, with a tractive effort of 30,740 lb., had the high-pressure cylinders (16½ in. diameter by 24 in. stroke) driving the rear group of coupled wheels, while the low-pressure cylinders, which were 26 in. diameter, drive the leading group. The coupled wheels were 3 ft. 6½ in. diameter, and the engine alone in working order weighed 86½ tons. It was an impressive sight to see one of the heavy mail trains from the Cape, including dining and sleeping cars, thundering up the gradients of the Hex River pass with one of the '15CA' 4-8-2 engines at its head (ref. 111) and a 'Mallet' assisting in rear. The electrification of the line through this difficult region made the Mallet banking engines redundant, and they have now all been scrapped.

37 Benguela Railway: 4-8-0 General Service Locomotive.

In referring to the Rhodesian 4-8-2 (ref. 35) mention was made of the popularity of the 4-8-0 type for general service in Southern Africa. The Benguela Railway, running inland from the Atlantic coast port of Lobito Bay through the Portuguese colony of Angola, has similar working conditions, and the 4–8–0 was introduced from the opening of the line in 1905. The interesting feature of the working is, however, the fuel used. Angola has no indigenous supplies either of coal or oil, and any locomotive fuel of such kind has to be imported. On the other hand, the eucalyptus tree makes excellent fuel. It grows freely, and so the production of these trees has been organized in a big way. For hundreds of miles along the line a belt of trees is grown. Felling is arranged on a cyclic basis, and except on a relatively short section near the coast, the entire railway is operated on wood-fired locomotives. The racks on the engine tenders are designed for the high stacking of logs. The 4–8–0 type of locomotive illustrated was introduced in 1923. It is a sturdy, straightforward design, having two cylinders 20 in. diameter by 24 in. stroke; coupled wheels 4 ft. 0 in. diameter, a total heating surface of 1498 sq. ft., and a boiler pressure of 160 lb. per sq. in.

38 South African Railways: The Pioneer Beyer–Garratt Locomotive.

Three locomotives of the type shown in our picture were ordered in 1914, but because of war conditions they were not delivered until 1920. The picture shows clearly the basic characteristics of the Garratt, with two separate engine units, and a single boiler carried on a central frame mounted on pivots on each of the engine units. The locomotive is thus articulated, and can negotiate sharp curves; the total weight is spread over a large number of axles, thus reducing the axle loading on the track, while the design of the central frame permits of a boiler of large diameter, without any encumbrance

from wheels or motion. The original South African 'Garratts' were for the narrow gauge (2 ft.) lines, principally in Natal, where the Stuartstown section, climbing to Donnybrook has a vertical rise of 4446 ft. in 98 miles. The ruling gradient is 1 in 33. On that line the heavier loads taken by the Garratt engine enabled the traffic to be worked with one less engine than previously. The engine illustrated is a tiny baby compared with the huge locomotives subsequently built on the Garratt principle, many of which are illustrated in this book. This pioneer South African engine had four cylinders $10\frac{1}{2}$ in. diameter by 16 in. stroke; coupled wheels 2 ft. 6 in. diameter, a total weight in working order of $48\frac{1}{4}$ tons, with a maximum axle load of 6·55 tons. The tractive effort at 85 per cent boiler pressure was 18,080 lb. How the principle was exploited within the short space of ten years is shown by references to the monster 'GL' Garratt of the South African Railways, illustrated under reference 66.

39 London, Midland and Scottish Railway: 'Cluster'-type Four-aspect Colour Light Signals, at Manchester.

The principle of railway colour light signals has become very familiar to the public at large by the adoption of the standard aspects—red for stop, amber for warning, and green for proceed—for road traffic signals. In the intense condition of railway working, and where there is a considerable disparity between the speed of the fastest and slowest trains, it was found necessary to introduce a fourth aspect—double yellow—as a preliminary warning. In its first application it was thought that the mounting of all four lenses of such a signal vertically would place the uppermost too high above drivers' eye level, and so the 'cluster' arrangement was devised. The disposition of the lenses starting from the top and travelling clockwise was yellow, red, yellow, green, so that one had the two yellows in a vertical line, as in a standard signal. The 'cluster' type was used only on the Southern Railway and at Manchester. The apprehension as to sighting which led to its being devised proved to be ill-founded, and use of the type was not perpetuated.

40 Great Western Railway: Reading, Semaphore Signals.

The Great Western Railway was the only one of the 'big four' in grouping days to retain the lower-quadrant semaphore signal as standard, but near to the end of the period covered by this book the detailed design of the semaphores themselves, and of the posts and fittings underwent considerable change. The old timber arms were replaced by a pressed-steel design, and the spectacles, which had hitherto been an elegant, though rather expensive, fabrication were changed to a one-piece casting. For many years the G.W.R. had used nothing but timber for all its signal posts; but the increasing difficulty, and cost, of obtaining good-quality timber led to the substitution of tubular steel masts, both for the main supports and for the 'doll' posts on which the actual semaphores are mounted. The bracket assembly shown in our picture illustrates a typical group, actually in the approach to Reading from the west on the Bristol main line. The signals relate to the relief line, and the semaphores reading from left to right control: entrance to goods yard; entry to up relief line platform; crossover road from up relief to up main line. The small distant arm mounted centrally on the post was for the guidance of train crews detaching slip coaches.

41 Southern Railway: Copyhold Junction, Colour Light Signals.

This is an interesting example of the use of one of the earliest forms of British colour light signal, with lenses showing the traditional green, amber, and red aspects. The particular example is to be found on the London-to-Brighton main line, at a junction with a branch line north of Haywards Heath. The interpretation of the colour displayed is different from those in road-traffic signals. The red commands a dead stop; the amber or yellow signifies that the next signal ahead is showing red, and although the driver of a train may pass the yellow, he must take immediate steps to reduce speed so that he can stop at the next signal. Green is the all-clear, and signifies 'full speed'. In the example shown there is a separate colour-light signal for each of the routes ahead, and the two pairs of signals relate, respectively, to two parallel tracks approaching the junction. The left-hand signal cleared indicates a route set for the left-hand route at the bifurcation, and vice versa. In more recent years the practice has developed of using a single colour-light signal, with an illuminated direction indicator mounted above it.

42 Great Western Railway: Cardiff, 'Searchlight' Signals.

In pre-nationalization days the Great Western was the only railway company not to adopt the new code of colour-light signalling, references 39 and 41. While taking advantage of the improved sighting qualities of light signals, the aspects adopted were exactly those of the former semaphore signalling practice. The signals shown in our picture are the precise equivalent of semaphore home and distant arms. The signal units themselves are of the so-called 'Searchlight' type, though the term 'searchlight' is more correctly a trade term rather than an exact description of the signal itself. In this type of signal a miniature electrical mechanism is built into the signal head, which enables different coloured beams to be projected from the one lens. In the signals shown in our picture the upper lenses display red or green, as required, while the lower lenses, following the code of semaphore signalling, display yellow or green. On other railways the 'Searchlight' type of signal was used in ordinary multi-aspect colourlight signalling and the units displayed were red, yellow, or green as required from the one lens. Where four aspects are required a separate light unit is mounted above the main. Searchlighttype colour-light signals are extensively used on overseas railways, including those of New Zealand, South Africa, and Rhodesia.

43 Great Western Railway: The 'Castle' Class Four-cylinder 4–6–0.

On the same page as the Milwaukee record-breaking 4–6–4 (ref. 46) it is appropriate to illustrate and describe its English rival in high-speed record breaking. Although the 'Castle' was introduced in 1923, its design was so successful that engines of the class continued to be built new up to the year 1939, with only detailed changes from the original drawings. Furthermore, from 1945 onwards, with modifications to the superheater and lubrication, many new engines of the same general class were built, until 1951. In some ways the 'Castle' was the very antithesis of contemporary American design, in that four cylinders were employed, and that the valve gear was inside the frames and completely hidden. The valves of the outside cylinders were

actuated by rocking shafts from the inside motion. The firebox was relatively small, designed to burn high-grade coal on a fairly deep firebed. The only point of precise similarity between the two locomotives was the boiler pressure of 225 lb. per sq. in. The 'Castles' were not only high-speed machines. They took turns on the heavy West of England expresses, which involved covering the first 95 miles out of London in 97 minutes with loads of 500 tons behind the tender. The four cylinders were 16 in. diameter by 26 in. stroke; the coupled wheels 6 ft. 8 in.; boiler pressure 225 lb. per sq. in., and the weight of engine and tender 126 tons. The tractive effort was 31,625 lb. The engine illustrated is the *Pendennis Castle*, No. 4079, one of the original batch of 1923, and now preserved under private ownership.

44 Northern Railway of France: A Chapelon 4–6–2 (ex-P.O. Midi).

If one were asked to point to a single design that was outstanding above all others in the entire history of the steam locomotive the choice could well fall upon the Chapelon Pacific. Accountancy-wise, this amazing product of 1930 was not a new engine, but a most thoroughgoing rebuild of one of the earliest designs of Pacific to run in Europe. In all except the chassis and wheels, however, it was new—incredibly new, in the plethora of advanced ideas packed into that reconstruction. Few if any locomotive designs have had such a wide influence on future practice in many parts of the world. André Chapelon, of the Paris Orleans–Midi Railway redesigned the steam circuit so as to facilitate the passage of vast quantities of steam, freely. The engine remained a compound, and every detail concerning the flow of steam was *internally* streamlined. There was no fancy outer casing; the secret of outstanding success lay in the steam passages, the valves, the boiler, and in the proportions of the chimney and blastpipe. The rebuilt, or rather transformed, engines went into traffic on the Orleans road when the overall speed limit in France was 120 km. per hour (74½ m.p.h.), and they proved capable of hauling almost any load at that maximum speed, uphill or down. Their introduction came at a time when much of the line was being electrified, but the fame of these engines spread throughout France, and far beyond too, and our picture shows one that had been acquired by the Northern Railway, and working on the fast expresses from Paris to Calais, for the English packet services, and to Lille. The last of these outstanding engines were only recently taken out of traffic on the boat trains from Calais and Boulogne.

45 **Pennsylvania Railroad:** The 'M1a' 4–8–2 Mixed Traffic Locomotive.

The Pennsylvania was always one of the most individualistic of all the American Railroads in steam locomotive design. Some of its specialities were mentioned in connection with the 'K4s' Pacific express passenger locomotives (ref. 23), such as the use of the Belpaire firebox. When it came to the production of a heavy mixed-traffic type, capable of dealing with fast freight, and also for handling the heaviest passenger trains over the Allegheny Mountain section—which includes the celebrated 'Horseshoe Curve'—it was no more than natural to develop the highly successful 'Pacific' into a 4–8–2. The 'M1a' illustrated is itself a development of the first Pennsylvania 4–8–2s. It has the characteristic Belpaire firebox, and a long combustion chamber ahead, and the actual boiler barrel contains comparatively short tubes.

The Pennsylvania Railroad has its own stationary testing plant at the Altoona Works, and features of design that proved very successful in service were developed by exhaustive experimenting on this plant. The 'M1a' engines had two cylinders 27 in. diameter by 30 in. stroke; coupled wheels 6 ft. in diameter thereby enabling them to undertake express passenger duties, while the boiler pressure was 250 lb. per sq. in., against 205 in the 'K4s' Pacifics. The total weight of engine and tender was 342 tons, against the 237 of the 'Pacifics', and the tractive effort 64,550 lb. During the year 1933 many of these locomotives were averaging nearly 5000 miles a month, in heavy freight service.

46 **Chicago, Milwaukee, St Paul, and Pacific Railroad:** Record-breaking 4–6–4 Express Locomotive.

The 1930s became a time of intense railway enterprise in many parts of the world, and the famous runs of the Great Western 'Cheltenham Flyer' in 1931 and 1932 temporarily captured the world speed record for a start-to-stop run. From 6 June 1932 this record stood at 81·7 m.p.h.—77·3 miles in 56 minutes 47 seconds. In the meantime the Milwaukee road was preparing for very fast services over the 85·7 miles between Chicago and Milwaukee, which eventuated in the introduction of the famous 'Hiawatha' express, and in July 1934 the ordinary 9 a.m. train from Chicago, normally allowed 90 min. for the run, was worked at extra high speed, by way of a trial. In relation to the weight of the engine the load was somewhat lighter than that of the Cheltenham Flyer: 408 tons of train, with an engine and tender of 326¾ tons. The Great Western weights were 186 and 126 tons respectively. For the first 12 miles out of

Chicago the speed was no more than moderate; but then a stretch of 65·6 miles was covered in a shade under 43 minutes, an average of 92·3 m.p.h. Near the end of this flying stretch a maximum of 103½ m.p.h. was attained, and although the start-to-stop average of 76·1 m.p.h. did not eclipse the Great Western record, which had the advantage of a very fast get-a-way, and a fast finish, the 'flying' average just quoted was superior. Our picture shows the locomotive concerned; a very large 4–6–4 of orthodox American design of the period, with two cylinders 26 in. diameter by 28 in. stroke; 6 ft. 8 in. coupled wheels, and a total weight in working order of 326¾ tons. The tractive effort was 45,822 lb.

47 Bengal Nagpur Railway: The Class 'N' 4–8–0 + 0–8–4 Beyer–Garratt Engine.

This railway, one of the last in India to remain under private ownership, operated a very heavy coal traffic, and with 1600-ton trains it had been necessary to double-head, with two of the standard 2–8–0 tender engines. In making the first experiments with the Beyer–Garratt type the engine units were made precisely the same as the existing tender engines, the valve motion being the same. The first Beyer–Garratts on the line were thus of the 2–8–0 + 0–8–2 type and precisely double the capacity of the existing 2–8–0. Experience with these engines led to the design of a larger and improved Garratt in which the 4–8–0 + 0–8–4 wheel arrangement was used. The Bengal Nagpur was the only railway to use this type. In their design advantage was taken of the 5 ft. 6 in. gauge standard on principal railways in India, and the maximum permitted axle load of 20 tons. The resulting locomotives were the largest

and heaviest ever to run in India, and have done splendid work with the very heavy coal trains. The four cylinders were 20½ in. diameter by 26 in. stroke; coupled wheels 4 ft. 8 in. diameter; the boiler had a total evaporative heating surface of 3404 sq. ft. and a superheating surface of 642 sq. ft.; the grate area is 69·8 sq. ft. and the working pressure 210 lb. per sq. in. The total weight in working order is 234 tons, and the tractive effort at 85 per cent boiler pressure, 69,700 lb. Our picture shows one of these engines in the handsome green livery of the Bengal Nagpur Railway.

48 Chesapeake and Ohio: 2–8–8–2 Simple Articulated Freight Engine.

Following the success of the single expansion, or 'simple', articulated engine, as distinct from the true Mallet, which was a compound, referred to in connection with the Baltimore and Ohio Class EL-5A 2–8–8–0 (ref. 24), the articulated type, with four cylinders all taking live steam, began to develop to enormous proportions in the U.S.A. As early as the year 1924 the American Locomotive Company (ALCO) built the class of gigantic 2–8–8–2s for the Chesapeake and Ohio Railroad, shown in our picture. This line was much concerned with the transport of coal over long and heavy gradients, and these engines with a tractive effort of no less than 103,500 lb. were ideally suited to the slow, hard, slogging duty associated with such traffic. The four cylinders were 23 in. diameter by 32 in. stroke, while the driving-wheel diameter was relatively small, 4 ft. 9 in. The boiler was enormous, with an evaporative heating surface of 6443 sq. ft., a superheating surface of 1885 sq. ft., and a grate area of 112·9 sq. ft. So closely did the outside diameter of the boiler approach the loading gauge that the air-compressor outfit for the Westinghouse brake had to be accommodated on the front of the smokebox. The total weight of engine and tender in working order was 345 tons.

49 **Great Western Railway:** 2–8–0 Heavy Mineral Locomotive.

The name of G. J. Churchward will be for ever renowned in the history of locomotive engineering, and the 2–8–0 mineral engine of the Great Western Railway provides an outstanding example of his development. In its earliest form it dates back to 1903, and it formed a major part of a great scheme of standardization in which boilers, cylinders, and valve motion were standard and interchangeable among a number of locomotive classes designed to work in a variety of traffics. Except in its wheel arrangement, the 2–8–0 was standard with the 4–6–0. But the reason for this basic design of 1903 appearing in the present volume is that it remained the standard freight engine, not only of the Great Western Railway but also of the Western Region of the nationalized British Railways for more than *sixty years*. The design was improved in detail and its efficiency enhanced by use of superheated steam. When the time came for trials to be carried out, in 1948, between five different designs, none of which had its origin earlier than 1935, this Great Western design of 1903, with the single addition of superheating, was able to compete on level terms with all the rest. It belongs, as a basic up-to-date design, as much to the 1920–40 period on British railways as to the decade of its origin.

50 **Great Indian Peninsular Railway:** 2–8–0 Heavy Freight Locomotive.

This railway was the third largest in India and had a route-mileage of 4000. At the end of the 1920s, although some considerable progress had been made with electrification, there were 1300 steam locomotives in service. Recent additions to the stock had included batches of the Indian standard types (refs. 83, 135, and 157); but much of the traffic was being operated by older engines, and of these the H/5, 2–8–0 freighter is a characteristic example. It is similar in general design to the 2–8–0 locomotives of other Indian railways, but retained a number of characteristic G.I.P.R. features, including for a time the handsome chocolate brown livery. These engines were designed to the recommendations of the British Engineering Standards Association, and gave very many years of arduous, trouble-free service. In general size and weight they were very similar to the Great Western 2–8–0 (ref. 49), though built to the Indian 5 ft. 6 in. gauge; the boiler pressure, however, 180 lb. per sq. in., was considerably lower, and the boiler itself was of conventional design, with a straight rather than a tapered barrel. A number of these engines were equipped for oil burning. The weights in working order were, engine $75\frac{1}{2}$ tons; tender (conveying 4500 gallons of water and 2000 gallons of oil) $62\frac{3}{4}$ tons.

51 **South African Railways:** The '15A' Mixed Traffic 4–8–2 Locomotive.

The very severe gradients on certain sections of the main lines in South Africa, particularly in the Hex River Pass and on the Natal main line, necessitated the use of eight-coupled locomotives from an early date. At first 4–8–0s were used, but as larger boilers were needed an advance was made to the 4–8–2. In the line of development the '15A' class engine, illustrated, marks a notable stage. This class was a large one, and many of them are still in service today. The majority have been rebuilt, but a particularly fine example of the original design is still in regular service at Port Elizabeth, Cape Province. These large engines, as originally built, had two cylinders 22 in. diameter by 28 in. stroke; coupled wheels 4 ft. 9 in. diameter, and a boiler having 2026 sq. ft. of evaporative heating surface, 549 sq. ft. of superheating surface, and a grate area of 40 sq. ft. In working order the engine weighs 92 tons, and the large bogie tender another 51 tons. The tractive effort is 32,980 lb. Despite their relative small coupled wheels, they were free- and fast-running engines, regularly working up to the maximum speed of 55 m.p.h. permitted on steam-operated lines of the South African Railways.

52 Nizam's Guaranteed State Railway: 2–8–0 Mixed-traffic Locomotive.

These neat and compact, yet powerful, locomotives were representative of the later stages of the wholly British influence on Indian locomotive practice. But for the cow-catchers and the louvred windows on cab and tender, they could have passed for a standard design on the British home railways. This interesting railway operated in the State of Hyderabad, in the very centre of India, and it connected with several of the larger systems on its various frontiers. Its full title was 'His Exalted Highness the Nizam's Guaranteed State Railway', but among the European railway community of India it was usually known simply as 'The Nizam's'. The management, including that of the locomotive department, was British, mostly trained on the home railways. The locomotive which is the subject of our picture was of a general-purpose type, equally useful in working heavy

passenger trains at moderate speeds, as in freight service. The cylinders were 22 in. diameter by 26 in. stroke; coupled wheels 4 ft. 8½ in. diameter, boiler pressure 180 lb. per sq. in. and tractive effort 34,070 lb. The total weight of engine and tender in working order was 121¼ tons.

53 International Sleeping Car Company: A European Standard Sleeping Car.

The operation of sleeping-car services on the continent of Europe, in years before the Second World War was established under the auspices of an independent company, which provided sleeping cars of a generally standard design for working on many international express trains. The livery, in royal blue with gold lettering, was the same throughout, but the inscriptions varied in accordance with the routes over which the cars were operating. The car in our picture has the company's name in French, while the inscription 'sleeping car' is in French at one entrance and in English at the other. It could equally have had inscriptions in Polish and been used on the through pre-war service between Paris and Warsaw. They are massive vehicles, of all-steel construction, and ride most luxuriously. By British standards, however, the berths are rather cramped. Whereas a two-berth cabin in Great Britain has two single berths at ground level, with a connecting door between the two, in the Continental *wagons-lit* the berths are arranged one above the other. Although most comfortable once you get into bed, it usually means one passenger taking a walk in the corridor while the other undresses and retires for the night. The appointments are nevertheless all very conveniently arranged.

54 Royal State Railways of Siam (now Thailand): Second- and Third-class Composite Carriage.

The train services on the railways of Thailand involve some lengthy runs both to the north and to the south of Bangkok, often made in extremely hot weather in a climate having a very high humidity figure. In 1929 the State Railway of Siam, as it was then known, introduced some fine new rolling stock for second- and third-class passengers, including the first all-steel coaches ever used in that country. At that time the management was evidently not convinced of the advantages to be derived from all-steel coaches, because out of an order for fifty new coaches placed with the Metropolitan Cammell Carriage Wagon and Finance Company, thirty were steel, and the remainder constructed with teak bodies. The carriage illustrated is a steel one, but it was a feature of the contract that externally the steel vehicles should resemble the teak ones as closely as possible, including the external finish. The interiors are of the open saloon type, except the coaches providing first-class accommodation. This latter is of the compartment type seating two aside. The composite carriage illustrated seats 48 third- and 18 second-class passengers. Although running on the metre gauge, the overall width of these carriages is 8 ft. $10\frac{5}{8}$ in.—almost as wide as in Great Britain.

55 London and North Eastern Railway: Tourist Train Buffet Car.

When the London and North Eastern Railway was formed, in 1923, three of the constituent companies finished their coaching stock by simply varnishing the natural timber used in the bodies, and on grouping the famous 'varnished teak' of the Great Northern Railway, as exemplified in our picture of the dining-car set (ref. 137) became standard for the new railway. Sir Nigel Gresley, as Chief Mechanical Engineer, was, however, not averse to departing from standard for both coaches and locomotives required for special duties, and in 1933 when some new train-sets, designed specially for tourist and day excursion traffic, were built he adopted an entirely new style. These coaches had steel underframes, and the body framing, as usual, was of teak; but the bodies were made flush sided with plywood panelling. The exterior finish was in L.N.E.R. engine green up to the waist line, and cream above. The complete-set trains consisted of 12 coaches, all third class and entirely of the open-saloon type, and two buffet cars were included. These trains became extremely popular.

56 Boston and Maine Railroad: Standard Passenger Car.

Towards the end of the First World War the Boston and Maine took delivery of the first all-steel cars to be used on that line, and they subsequently became a standard type for many years. They were introduced for the through express-train service between New York and Portland, and were very massively constructed. This was a considerable time before the use of welding for the fabrication of steel frameworks, and all the joints were riveted. They seated 88 passengers in reversible seats, two passengers on each side of the central gangway. The interior was spacious, but savoured more of a 'tram' rather than a main-line railway carriage. Despite the large amount of seating, the car was heavy in relation to the number of passengers, weighing $53\frac{1}{2}$ tons. This nevertheless represented a considerable reduction in weight when comparison was made with the similar cars of other American railroads. The New York Central, for example, had a number of cars also 70 ft. long, and seating 84 passengers, of which the tare weight was no less than 63 tons. These latter cars had six-wheeled bogies, whereas the Boston and Maine car illustrated had four-wheeled bogies. The weights make an interesting comparison with the G.W.R. stock (ref. 11); 80 passengers; 37 tons tare.

57 Chesapeake and Ohio: Bogie Coal Car.

This railway handled a very large tonnage of export coal from the West Virginia and Kentucky fields, and to facilitate the handling of such traffic the pier at Newport News was equipped with a pair of stationary turn-over car dumpers, each of which was capable of handling all sizes of cars up to 100 tons, and, moreover, at a rate of 30 cars per hour. To take full advantage of this remarkable capacity for loading the ships at the pier, the Chesapeake and Ohio put into service, as a single order, no fewer than 1000 of the huge gondola-type coal cars illustrated in our picture. The inside dimensions were, length 43 ft. 3 in.; width 10 ft. $1\frac{1}{2}$ in.; height 7 ft. $5\frac{1}{2}$ in. Fully loaded with coal heaped at an angle of 30 deg. from the outside edges, this gave a capacity of 100 tons—short tons, that is, of 2000 lb. In English tons the load was 89 tons. The tare weight of the car was $30\frac{1}{2}$ English tons. The cars were stencilled on their sides to carry a pay-load of 182,000 lb., 81 tons; the difference between this and the 89 tons maximum was designed to provide for overloading. The cars were, of course, fitted with continuous automatic brakes,

and arrangements for varying the braking force to suit 'empty' and 'load' conditions. The difference between 'tare' and 'maximum' load was between $30\frac{1}{2}$ and $119\frac{1}{2}$ tons.

58 Great Western Railway: 120-ton Trolley Wagon.

In the 1930s it was still customary to transport very heavy special loads by rail. Sometimes the individual objects to be conveyed were so large as to overhang the gauge. Then special arrangements had to be made for conveyance on Sundays, with one track of a double-line main route closed to other traffic in order to accommodate the overhang. The vehicle illustrated was designed and built at Swindon specially for conveying heavy electrical gear, such as transformers, and the design was carried out in consultation with the Central Electricity Board. The two main girders which carried the load were supported at the ends by swivelling cross bolsters, to which were attached the top halves of the main pivots. The bottom halves were supported on special frames carried on two six-wheeled bogies. Thus to convey one of these huge transformers, or similar gear, a railway vehicle having 24 wheels was required. The whole outfit had a total length of 89 ft. 6 in. over buffers, and had a tare weight of 76 tons. With the maximum permissible paying load of 120 tons the entire equipage had the weight of a fair-sized train, 196 tons. Our picture shows the arrangements for pivoting, and indicates how readily the equipage could negotiate relatively sharp curves.

59 Atchison, Topeka, and Santa Fé: Double-deck Stock Car.

An interesting example of the numerous attempts to secure more economical transportation, with greater pay-loads for the same tare weight, was to be seen in the use of double-deck cars for livestock on the Santa Fé. The generous height of the American loading gauge permitted of two decks in cars designed for conveyance of sheep and other livestock. Their chief feature, however, was that the upper deck was movable. It rested on a belt rail, and could be raised by an arrangement of chains and winding shaft when the car was required to be used for one deck only. The length inside was 40 ft., with an inside width of 8 ft. 8 in. When the upper deck was lowered the distance from the floor to the bottom of the upper deck was 3 ft. 7 in., and there was the same space between the upper deck and the underside of the carlines. With the deck in the raised position the distance between the floors and the underside of the deck was 6 ft. 10 in. As such the cars could be used for a variety of purposes, and at one time the Santa Fé had many hundreds of them in use. Their tare weight was 21 tons, and the maximum pay-load was registered as 36 tons.

60 **Pennsylvania Railroad:** 85-ton Hopper Car.

This interesting vehicle provides yet another example of the high-capacity freight cars introduced in the U.S.A. in the early 1920s. It provides an interesting contrast to the Chesapeake and Ohio car described under reference 59. The Pennsylvania Railroad had no direct export traffic, delivered in its own vehicles to seaports, and although it carried an enormous volume of coal, it was practically all for internal use. The design of cars was thus arranged to suit the discharge facilities, and these, in many localities, consisted of dumping from high-level gantries. These cars were therefore arranged for bottom discharge, from hopper doors. The cars were of all-steel construction, and had five pairs of doors. They were designed and built at the Pennsylvania Railroad's own shops at Altoona. The cars were of very large proportions, having an overall length over the end sills of 48 ft. 4 in., and a tare weight of 27 English tons. Because of the hopper form of construction, and the need to slope the ends so that the coal trimmed readily the total capacity is not so great as that of a gondola car. The official designation '85-ton' refers to 'short' tons. In English measure the capacity was 76 tons.

61 **London, Midland and Scottish Railway:** Aisgill Signal Box.

The small-town or country signal box on British railways in the era of semaphore signalling was usually a highly distinctive building. Each of the different companies had their own individual style, and the majority of these were little works of art. Some companies used timber throughout, others a mixture of brick, or stone and timber work, while others built highly massive erections that looked as though they had been designed to withstand a siege! With mechanical signalling, and on main lines a signal box every two or three miles along the route, the equipment in each box was relatively small, and operated by a single man, entirely on his own for an eight-hour shift. Although the routines were most comprehensively laid down, it was a responsible job. The box illustrated in our picture is of the Midland Railway type, constructed in timber. It is situated in a very lonely place on the borders of Yorkshire and Westmorland in wild fell country, at the very summit point of the line between London (St Pancras) and

Carlisle, 1151 ft. above sea-level. The adjacent signal boxes are 3 miles on either side. In steam days one of its most important functions was to regulate movements concerned with the detaching of assistant engines from heavy trains which had required double-heading up the long inclines leading to this lofty summit point.

62 London, Midland and Scottish Railway: Toton Marshalling Yard Signal Box.

Our picture shows a totally different architectural style in signal-box construction, although belonging to the same railway administration as Aisgill. This large box controls traffic movements into and out of one of the largest marshalling areas in the country, the southern extremity of this South Nottinghamshire coalfield. The equipment inside, though far more extensive, is similar to that of Aisgill, with full-sized mechanical levers, and rod working for the points, but as will be seen, the box is built entirely of brick, and in a contemporary 'square' type of architecture. The first stages in the modernization of working in the approaches to the Toton yards were carried out in the late 1930s, when the threat of a second world war was becoming even more serious. Protection of vital equipment against the risk of air-raid damage became an important consideration in all new railways works, and signal boxes, if built in the former traditional style of the Midland Railway, in timber, would have been particularly vulnerable. Of course, even a massive brick building such as that illustrated would not have been proof against a direct hit, but the protection against blast, and minimizing of fire risks was greatly enhanced.

63 Delft, 'Post U': Dutch Signal Box.

In Great Britain the signal box in mechanical days, regardless of the materials in which it was constructed, had a certain definite *motif* in design. It had a 'villa' or 'chalet' appearance, and although some boxes in special localities had unusual aspects, these were the exceptions rather than the rule. On the continent of Europe, however, although the majority of countries were slower off the mark than Great Britain in adopting colour-light signalling, there was, by the beginning of the 1930s, a marked change towards a much more modern style of architecture, even though the operating methods remained the same. The Dutch, like many Continental countries, used the double-wire system of point operation. There were no heavy down-rods from the interlocking frame to ground level; instead the scheme of things could be described as an endless rope, in which an operating wheel at the actual points was connected to another one in the signal cabin. The former rotated in synchronization with the movements imparted to the latter by the signalman. With no heavy down rods to accommodate, the light and airy form of signal-box construction could be readily adopted.

64 Southern Railway: Bickley Junction Signal Box.

This interesting box formed one of a series at the intersection of two important main lines out of London: the South-Eastern, starting from Charing Cross and coming by way of New Cross and Hither Green, and the London Chatham and Dover, via Herne Hill and Bromley. Before the working union of the two companies in 1899 the Chatham line passed beneath the South-Eastern just on the country side of Chislehurst. It was one of the major developments following the working union that a series of inter-connecting junctions between the two main lines was constructed, and Bickley Junction, on the Chatham line, marked the point of bifurcation of the connecting line to the South-Eastern, extensively used by boat express trains, originating at Victoria. The signal box was built in the Chatham style, in yellow brick, and very substantially constructed. The railway itself, constantly in the direst financial straits, did not skimp matters when it came to signalling equipment, and in the nineteenth century its practice was some of the most advanced anywhere in the world. Our picture shows the box as it was modified for war service. The windows in the lower storey, providing light for maintenance of the heavy mechanical underfloor equipment, were bricked up as a precaution against possible air-raid damage.

65 **South African Railways:** The Giant 'MH' Class 2–6–6–2 Mallet Articulated Compound.

Whereas the 'MJ' class Mallets (ref. 36) were introduced primarily for assisting trains on difficult stretches of line, such as in the Hex River pass, the enormous engines that are the subject of our present picture were essentially main-line heavy freight engines designed particularly for the Natal main line, where between Durban and Cato Ridge there is a vertical rise of 2449 ft. in 45 miles, an average inclination of 1 in 95. But the most severe section includes a very long stretch at 1 in 66, and the giant Mallet compound engines were designed to haul freight trains of 500 tons up this incline. These engines were of immense length for the 3 ft. 6 in.

gauge, and weighed 128 tons without the tender. The total weight was 179 tons. The tractive effort was 48,000 lb. when working full compound, but the equipment included a change valve enabling the driver to admit live steam to all four cylinders for short periods. These engines, of which five were built in 1915, were eventually superseded by the Beyer–Garratt articulated type, of which the 'GL' class (ref. 66) could haul a load double that of the Mallets. As an example of British locomotive construction at the beginning of the period covered by this book the 'MH' Mallet is outstanding.

66 **South African Railways:** The 'GL' Class 4–8–2 + 2–8–4 Beyer–Garratt Freight Engine.

The main line of the former Natal Government Railways is one of the most severely graded in all Africa. The original route inland from Durban included gradients of 1 in 30, and although a realigned route was later built at great expense, it nevertheless included 38 miles almost continuously at 1 in 66. Proposals to electrify it were made as long ago as 1914, but were delayed by the war, and by the late 1920s the question of motive power had become serious, because the heaviest freight trains required two powerful 4–8–2 tender engines. A truly monster Garratt was therefore planned, which would do the work of the two 4–8–2s, and the new engine was literally, so far as wheel arrangement went, two 4–8–2s. An enormous boiler had to be provided to feed *two* such engine units, which had altogether four cylinders 22 in. diameter by 26 in. stroke. That boiler had an evaporative heating surface of 3376 sq. ft., a superheating surface of 809 sq. ft. and a grate area of 74·5 sq. ft. The diameter of the boiler barrel was just twice the rail gauge—7 ft. The total weight of the engine is 211 tons, and the tractive effort, at 85 per cent boiler pressure, 89,000 lb. On the bank from Durban to Cato Ridge the maximum load worked by the standard 4–8–2 tender engines was 500 tons, and on a comparative test one of these engines climbed the bank in 184 minutes. The 'GL' Garratt, working at some way below full capacity, took a load of 1117 tons up in 163 minutes, and on the following day the still heavier load of 1205 tons was successfully worked. The new engines were thus well over double the capacity of the 4–8–2 tender engines.

67 Kenya and Uganda Railway: The 'EC2' Class Beyer–Garratt Locomotive.

The Kenya and Uganda is essentially a mountain line, climbing from sea-level at Mombasa to over 5500 ft. at the head-quarters at Nairobi, and then to just over 9000 ft. at the summit point at Timboroa, near which the line crosses the Equator. The line was laid with relatively light permanent way, and to save expensive earthworks the alignment is exceedingly curving in places. These two physical features, combined with the existence on many stretches of long, gruelling inclines at 1 in 50, made the provision of adequate motive power very difficult for operating the traffic. With long stretches of single line it was necessary to make the traffic offered into long trains, and the Beyer–Garratt type of articulated locomotive provided, virtually, two locomotives in one. The rail gauge is one metre, and on no section could axle loads of more than 11¾ tons be permited; but by the use of 4–8–2 + 2–8–4 wheel arrangement, a locomotive having a tractive effort of 40,000 lb. was provided. To supply four cylinders 16½ in. diameter by 22 in. stroke

a large boiler was necessary, and the Garratt principle permitted of ideal dimensions—namely a large diameter and short barrel. The grate area was 43·6 sq. ft., and this was, of course, not beyond the range of hand firing. The engine illustrated in our picture has the additional feature of a feed-water heater on the boiler. There were, before the war, 36 engines of this type, and in the year 1937 they ran a total of 1,581,427 miles. Considering the slowness of running on the tremendous mountain gradients, the average of 43,928 miles per year per engine for the entire stud consti-tuted something of a record for mountain operation on the metre gauge.

68 Southern Pacific Lines: The Cab-in-front 4–8–8–2 of 1928.

The main line of the Southern Pacific between Sparks, Nevada, and Roseville, California, a distance of 139 miles, follows the historic Overland Trail across the summit of the Sierra Nevada mountains. The railway climbs to an altitude of 7000 ft. above sea-level, and on the west-bound run the ruling gradient is 1 in 40 for nearly 85 miles. Locomotives of immense power are needed for working heavy trains over such a route, and in 1928 a first batch of these enormous articulated type engines was placed with the Baldwin Locomotive Works. They were oil-fired, and to give the drivers a good lookout the engine is turned back to front as it were, with the fuel tank trailing behind. Al-though built on the Mallet articulated principle, these engines are not com-pounds, and have four cylinders, 24 in. diameter by 32 in. stroke, all taking live steam from the boiler. The working pres-sure is 235 lb. per sq. in., and in conjunc-tion with coupled wheels of 5 ft. 3½ in. diameter provides a tractive effort of

112,760 lb. The boiler is understandably enormous, having an evaporative heating surface of 6505 sq. ft. and a superheating surface of 2988 sq. ft. The grate area is 139 sq. ft. The total weight of engine and tender in working order is 403 tons. These enormous engines work trailing loads of 2000 tons on a 1 in 66 at 16–17 m.p.h.; while on the truly killing stretches of 1 in 40 ascent they maintain much the same speed, with a reduced load of about 1350 tons. This, of course, was tremendous haulage on such a gradient.

69 **Great Northern Railway of Ireland:** Three-cylinder Compound 4–4–0 Locomotive.

This efficiently managed railway, with its main line running between Dublin and Belfast, became a truly International route, with customs examination at the frontier stations of Goraghwood and Dundalk. But although there was this separation, one locomotive worked through from end to end. Three sheds were involved, Dublin, Dundalk, and Belfast, and the manning of the locomotives was shared between these three. Dublin and Belfast men worked only as far as Dundalk, but the Dundalk men worked sometimes to Dublin and sometimes to Belfast. The new compound engines were introduced in 1932, and so far as general proportions and capacity were concerned were very similar to the English Midland compounds. At first they were painted plain black, but then the beautiful bright blue livery was introduced. They were always kept spotlessly clean, and proved themselves powerful and fast runners. On the fast stretches of line in Eire between Dublin and Drogheda speeds of 75–80 m.p.h. were frequent, while on the descent from Adavolye summit to Dundalk the speed was often

85 m.p.h. or more. Appropriately the engines of this class were named after some of the fastest flying birds: *Eagle*, *Falcon*, *Merlin*, *Peregrine*, and *Kestrel*.

70 **Great Southern Railway (Eire):** Two-cylinder 4–6–0 Express Locomotive.

The introduction of 4–6–0 locomotives for express passenger service on the former Great Southern and Western Railway was fraught with much difficulty. The design was based on that of the Great Western 'Star' class, and was a four-cylinder machine; but certain features were not satisfactory, and in the late 1920s a start was made with rebuilding the original engines as two-cylinder machines. With the much simpler layout of machinery, and improvements in detail design a successful engine was produced which, with certain variations between individual locomotives, hauled the traffic until the advent of Mr Bredin's '800' class engines in 1939 (ref. 72). Three of the original four-cylinder engines were scrapped in 1929–30, and the remaining seven, all rebuilt with two cylinders, did excellent work. Two were fitted with the Caprotti valve gear, and a final development was the fitting of larger boilers. Our picture shows No. 401, fitted with Caprotti valve gear—a very fast and economical engine. As thus rebuilt the leading dimensions were: cylinders, 19½ in. diameter by 28 in. stroke; coupled wheels 6 ft. 7 in. diameter, boiler pressure 180 lb. per sq. in., total weight in working order 122 tons.

71 **L.M.S.R. Northern Counties Committee (Ireland):** 2–6–0 Express Passenger Locomotive.

Until the year 1933 passenger-train service from Belfast to the North Atlantic coast and to Londonderry had been handicapped by the need to reverse direction at Greenisland and restart up a severe incline. The completion of the new loop line enabled direct running to be made from Belfast to the north, and in readiness for accelerated services the type of 2–6–0 illustrated was introduced. It was based on the standard L.M.S.R. 2–6–4 tank engine, and had the same extremely efficient layout of the Walschaerts valve gear. The leading dimensions were, cylinders 19 in. diameter by 26 in. stroke; coupled wheels 6 ft. diameter, and total weight including tender $95\frac{1}{2}$ tons. The nine engines of the class were built between 1933 and 1936, and all were named; the engine in our picture, completed in 1935, was named in honour of the Silver Jubilee of King George V. They were extremely smooth- and free-running engines, and they worked trains of seven and eight heavy corridor coaches on the 'North Atlantic Express' and the 'Portrush Flyer' with notable economy. These trains involved covering the 68 miles between Belfast and Portrush in 80 minutes over a route including a high proportion of single track.

72 **Great Southern Railway (Eire):** Three-cylinder 4–6–0 Express Locomotive, *Maeve*.

The main line of the Great Southern system between Dublin and Cork had, throughout the period between the two world wars, been subject to a steady increase in traffic. There was ordinary business, centred upon the working of the English mail trains, tourist traffic to and from the highly scenic south-west of Ireland, and the periodic special workings in connection with the calling of transatlantic liners at Cobh. To meet the requirements of heavier trains, Mr E. C. Bredin designed a magnificent new 4–6–0 express locomotive, of which the first example was put into traffic just before the Second World War. Breaking away from a long tradition of unlined black engines, No. 800, named *Maeve*, was finished in a very handsome livery of light bluish green with black-and-white lining. She was by far the most powerful engine to run in Ireland, and completely eliminated the need for double-heading and indeed of triple-heading on the very severe incline out of Cork. The leading dimensions were, cylinders (three) $18\frac{1}{2}$ in. diameter by 28 in. stroke; coupled wheels 6 ft. 7 in. diameter; grate area $33\frac{1}{2}$ sq. ft.; boiler pressure 250 lb. per sq. in.; total weight of engine and tender in working order 135 tons; tractive effort at 85 per cent boiler pressure 33,000 lb. At the end of 1939 two further engines of the same design were built at Inchicore Works, and named *Macha* and *Tailte*. These pleasing Gaelic titles were those of ancient queens of Ireland.

73 **New Zealand Government Railways:** The Class 'Ab' 'Pacific' of 1915.

This outstanding 3 ft. 6 in. gauge express passenger locomotive design dates from a time a little before the general period of this book, but it formed such a standard feature of passenger-train operating in New Zealand during one period that one could hardly think of omitting it purely on grounds of date of origin. Until the introduction of the very much larger 'K' class 4–8–4s (ref. 75) the 'Ab' class handled all the main-line passenger workings, and most of the main-line goods as well. They were very free running, and in their prime occasionally exceeded 60 m.p.h. They were the first in New Zealand to have the Vanderbilt-type of tender, with the water contained in a cylindrical tank. The leading dimensions were, cylinders 17 in. diameter by 26 in. stroke; coupled-wheel diameter 4 ft. 6 in.; boiler pressure 180 lb. per sq. in. The total weight of engine and tender in working order was 86·8 tons. At its maximum strength the class numbered 141, 38 of which were built by the New Zealand Railways, 83 by the North British Locomotive Company, and 20 by the firm of A. & G. Price.

74 New Zealand Government Railways: The 'Wab' Class 4–6–4 Tank Engine of 1917.

The success of the 'Ab' class main-line 'Pacific' engines led to the production of a tank engine version, and like the 'Ab' class, the first examples were produced at the railway shops at Addington. These massive and impressive-looking engines were designed for suburban passenger working around Auckland and Wellington, where the commuters' trains loaded up to fifteen cars, and speeds of 40–45 m.p.h. had to be attained between stops. The machinery of these engines was identical with that of the 'Ab' class, but the large side tanks and their load of water provided extra adhesion weight, and it was possible to have an increased tractive effort, by using higher boiler pressure, without increasing the risk of slipping. In the 'Wab' tank engines the pressure was 200 lb. per sq. in. They were also used for short-haul main-line passenger and freight working, and until the introduction of the 'K' class 4–8–4s a number of them were at work on the mountainous section of the North Island main line between Taihape and Taumarunui.

75 New Zealand Government Railways: The 'K' Class 4–8–4 of 1932.

By the end of the 1920s it was evident that larger locomotives than the 'Ab' Pacifics would be required for the heaviest and fastest service on the North Island main line, and it was decided that no half-hearted enlargement should be made. The new locomotives were to be at least 50 per cent more powerful than the 'Ab'. So there emerged from the Hutt workshops the giant 4–8–4 which is the subject of our picture. It was a very clever piece of engine designing, for a tractive effort of 30,815 lb. was obtained from a locomotive having a maximum axle load of only 14 tons. Of course, the limitation in overall height to 11 ft. 6 in. necessitated a somewhat 'squat' appearance, and seen by itself, the engine looks extraordinarily massive and comparable with some of the great American locomotives of the day. Actually the weight of the engine alone is only 86¾ tons—little more than an L.M.S.R. 'Royal Scot'. The cylinders were 20 in. diameter by 26 in. stroke; coupled-wheel diameter 4 ft. 6 in. and boiler pressure 200 lb. per sq. in. They were fast runners, and topped 60 m.p.h. frequently. Thirty of these splendid engines were put into service between 1932 and 1936.

76 New Zealand Government Railways: The 'J' Class Streamlined 4–8–4

While the 'K' class had very satisfactorily solved the problem of operation on the principal main lines, enhanced motive power was needed for the lines laid with rails weighing no more than 55 lb. per yard. The success of the 'K' class was such that the 4–8–4 wheel arrangement was becoming a favourite in New Zealand, so a light-weight version was designed, and a contract for 40 placed with the North British Locomotive Company in 1939. Although war had broken out before the consignment was completed, despite the hazards of shipment, all of them had arrived safely in New Zealand, after the long voyage from Scotland. They were designed to a maximum axle load of only $11\frac{1}{2}$ tons. The cylinders were 18 in. diameter by 26 in. stroke; coupled wheels 4 ft. 6 in. diameter, and boiler pressure 200 lb. per sq. in. Many features were built into these engines to reduce weight, including coupling and connecting rods of high-tensile alloy steel. The use of 'stream-lining' was something of a 'gimmick' for branch-line engines that rarely exceeded 50 m.p.h. in ordinary service, and some of the sheathing was removed later to facilitate maintenance. They were excellent engines, and proved very popular with all concerned.

77 Kenya and Uganda Railway: The Giant 'EC3' Class 4–8–4 + 4–8–4 Beyer–Garratt Locomotive.

The problem of line occupation on this mountain railway was becoming a matter of serious concern towards the end of the 1930s, and the only way to get more traffic through seemed to be to run longer trains and maintain higher average speeds. The 'EC2' Garratt engines (ref. 67) had coupled wheels only 3 ft. 7 in. diameter, for coping with the heavy gradients. It was felt that better running might be made on the easier sections with larger coupled wheels, though at the same time enhanced tractive power was needed. Thus there eventuated the remarkable 'EC3' class, the first locomotives in the world to have the 4–8–4 + 4–8–4 wheel arrangement. The cylinders were enlarged to 16 in. diameter by 26 in. stroke; the coupled wheels were

made 4 ft. 6 in. diameter, and the enormous boiler had a firegrate area of $48\frac{1}{2}$ sq. ft. Even so, they remained hand fired. The crews consisted of European or Asian drivers with African firemen, and the locomotives were manned on the caboose system. Two crews travelled on the train, one resting in the caboose while the other worked the locomotive. In comparing the overall weight of these large locomotives, $186\frac{1}{4}$ tons, with some of their American contemporaries, illustrated elsewhere in this book, the limitations of the metre gauge must be borne in mind, and one can only admire the outstanding skill in design that produced such a locomotive while having no axle load greater than $11\frac{3}{4}$ tons. The tractive effort was 46,100 lb. In addition to working on the mail trains between Mombasa and Nairobi in connection with ocean-liner sailings, these engines made regular round trips of 1000 miles from Nairobi to the western end of the line in Uganda, at Kampala.

78 Denver and Rio Grande Western: The 4–6–6–4 Simple Articulated Freight Locomotive.

The very name of this railway suggests romance of the wild country of the Rocky Mountains. But wild country and awe-inspiring mountain scenery inevitably means very hard going for the railway engineer, both in the maintenance of a severely graded and sharply curved track and in the provision of adequate locomotive power. Furthermore, in a competitive world freight trains could not afford to lumber along on the easy stretches; they must be worked through the mountain passes at something approaching passenger-train speed, and it was to meet the needs of heavy hill-climbing, and reasonably fast running on the more favourable stretches that the remarkable design shown in our picture was evolved. It has the same tractive effort as the Chesapeake and Ohio coal engine (ref. 48), but with driving wheels of 5 ft. 10 in. diameter it could run a maximum-tonnage freight train at 65-70 m.p.h. where track conditions permitted. In this Baldwin product of 1938 the cylinders were 23 in. diameter by 32 in. stroke; the boiler had 6341 sq. ft. of evaporative heating surface, a superheating surface of 2628 sq. ft. and a grate area of 136·5 sq. ft. The boiler pressure was 255 lb. per sq. in. against 205 in the C. & O. engine, and the total weight in working order was a modest 460 tons!

79 Southern Railway (England): The 'Schools' Class Three-cylinder 4-4-0.

The 'King Arthur' class of 4-6-0 (ref. 9), of which there were 74, were in the late 1920s considered the standard express passenger engine of the Southern Railway. It is true that 16 larger 4-6-0s of the 'Lord Nelson' class were also at work, but these were reserved for specially arduous tasks. When additional motive power was needed for the Hastings line, which is severely graded, structural clearances in some of the tunnels near Tunbridge Wells precluded the use of the 'King Arthurs' and a new design of 4-4-0 was worked out, which was a synthesis of existing parts and tools that were available. By using three out of the four cylinders of a 'Lord Nelson', and their associated valve gear, an engine unit of the required power could be obtained; but weight restrictions precluded use of the large Belpaire firebox of the 'Nelsons', so the 'King Arthur' boiler was taken instead, shortened in the barrel to suit the 4-4-0 chassis. The result was the finest 4-4-0 ever to run in Great Britain,

and one of the best engine classes on the Southern Railway. Their use was not confined to the Hastings line, and in later years they did magnificent work on the Bournemouth expresses. Their names, 40 in all, were those of famous English public schools. The engine illustrated, No. 925, *Cheltenham*, is shown in the Bulleid livery of Malachite green. When first built they were finished in olive green, as shown in the 'King Arthur' (ref. 9). Their leading dimensions were cylinders (three) $16\frac{1}{2}$ in. diameter by 26 in. stroke; coupled wheels 6 ft. 7 in. diameter; heating surfaces, evaporative 1766 sq. ft., superheater 283 sq. ft.; grate area 28·3 sq. ft.; boiler pressure 220 lb. per sq. in.; tractive effort 25,130 lb.

80 Egyptian State Railways: 4-4-0 Express Passenger Locomotive.

This is an interesting example of a light-weight medium-powered passenger locomotive designed to work over routes where the axle load is limited, and where a power unit of maximum efficiency is needed. At the time of their introduction in the mid-1930s the influence on the Egyptian State Railways was still almost entirely British, and although the absence of a steam dome lessens the likeness to any contemporary British design, all the main features, including plate frames and a general absence of external gadgets, are typical. Caprotti valve gear, with which these engines were equipped, was being used to an increasing extent in England at the time. The cylinders were 17 in. diameter by 26 in. stroke; coupled-wheel diameter was 5 ft. $6\frac{3}{4}$ in. and boiler pressure 180 lb. per sq. in. The total weight of the engine only in working order was only $54\frac{1}{2}$ tons, and the tractive effort 15,200 lb.

The boiler had top feed, as in standard Great Western practice; but the valves on top of the boiler had no ornamental covering, and the appearance of the engine suffered somewhat in consequence. The tender had a capacity for 3700 gallons of water and 6 tons of coal, and weighed $43\frac{1}{2}$ tons in working order.

81 **Northern Railway of France:** 4-4-2 de Glehn Compound with Lemaitre Front-end.

When they were first introduced at the turn of the century the de Glehn compound 4-4-2s of the Northern Railway of France took the railway world by storm, by the astonishing merit of their performance. Thirty-five years later one of them was selected for a remarkable modernization. It was a time when much research was in progress towards the improvement in efficiency, and certain of this work centred upon producing a freer exhaust. By this means not only would the back pressure be reduced, leading to a reduction in coal consumption, but the engine would run more freely. One improved exhaust system, which was more widely adopted, incidentally, in England than in France was that of Lemaitre, using a blastpipe consisting of a series of small jets instead of the single large one on a conventional locomotive. The outside sign of the Lemaitre exhaust system was an unusually large-diameter chimney tapering outwards from the base like a flower pot. The modernized French 'Atlantic', shown in our picture in the livery of the French National Railways, did some splendid work. For a time she was allocated to the 'Blue Bird' Pullman express running non-stop between Paris and Brussels at an average speed of 60 m.p.h.

82 **Great Northern Railway of Ireland:** Modernized 4-4-0 Simple Locomotive.

In the 1930s locomotive modernization often had an ominous ring about it, so far as the outward appearance of steam locomotives were concerned. In the cause of accessibility and to simplify maintenance, wheel splashers and low running plates, which had contributed so much to the neat and handsome appearance of earlier British locomotives, were removed; outside valve gear was introduced, and appurtenances hung on outside. On the Great Northern of Ireland, however, a thorough-going modernization of the Glover superheater 4-4-0s was carried out within the existing façade. There were structural improvements, but the factor contributing most to the enhancement of performance was a redesign of the valve gear. The Stephenson's link motion inside the frames was retained, but given a modern setting, though the outward lineaments of the locomotives were unchanged. When first introduced by Mr Glover in 1913 these engines were painted green. Then came the black era, but on rebuilding in the late 1930s they re-emerged in the beautiful blue of the compounds. In their rebuilt form they were immensely popular, and for a time took over the principal express workings between Dublin and Belfast.

83 **Indian Broad Gauge Standard:** The 'XB' 'Pacific' Class.

In 1924 the first Indian Locomotive Standard Committee was set up with the duty of drawing up a series of standard designs that could be used on any of the Indian railways. At that time not all the railways were Government owned. The Bengal Nagpur was a notable exception.

But the Committee was charged with making provision for the needs of great lines, such as the East Indian, the Great Indian Penninsular, the North Western, and certain smaller lines that had considerable broad-gauge mileage. An early decision was taken to adopt the 'Pacific' type, because it permitted of the use of wide boxes and large grate areas suitable for dealing with lower grades of coal. Three class of 'Pacific' were designed: the 'XA', a light engine with a maximum axle load of 13 tons; the 'XB' a general-service main-line type with a high route availability, and the 'XC', a heavy express passenger job. Our picture under this reference shows an 'XB' Pacific, one of a series fitted with feed-water heaters. This class had two cylinders $21\frac{1}{2}$ in. diameter by 28 in. stroke; coupled wheels 6 ft. 2 in.; a grate area of 45 sq. ft. and boiler pressure 180 lb. per sq. in. The total weight of engine and tender in working order is $155\frac{1}{4}$ tons, and the tractive effort 26,760 lb.

84 Bengal Nagpur Railway: The 'GSM' Class 4–6–0 Mail Engine.

In the late 1930s this railway, the locomotive practice of which stood quite apart from the general line of development in India, as exemplified by the 'XB' and 'XS' standard 'Pacifics' (refs. 83 and 85), designed and purchased from Robert Stephenson and Hawthorns Ltd. two very fine new 4–6–0 engines specially for the mail trains. They were designed to a maximum axle load of 17 tons, and had a tractive effort slightly greater than that of the 'XB' Pacifics of Indian standard design. In contrast to the 'Pacifics', the 'GSM' class had a very short boiler barrel, 13 ft. 6 in. between the tube plates, as against 18 ft. 6 in. on the standard 'Pacifics'; but the diameter was large, and all the

various ratios were conducive to a very free-steaming boiler. The firebox also was relatively small in grate area, but admirable in proportions for burning coal at a high firing rate if necessary. The locomotives generally were of advanced design, and gave excellent service. The cylinders were $21\frac{1}{2}$ in. diameter by 26 in. stroke; coupled-wheel diameter 6 ft. $1\frac{1}{2}$ in., and although the engine alone weighed no more than 75 tons, the tractive effort of 27,787 lb. was greater than that of the compound 'Pacifics' (ref. 86) which weighed 105 tons without their tenders.

85 North Western Railway (India): Class 'XS2' Four-cylinder 'Pacific' Express Locomotive.

In connection with the standard 'XB' type of Indian Pacific locomotive (ref. 83), reference was also made to the 'XA' and 'XC' standard designs, both of which are of the two-cylinder type. In 1928 the Indian Railway Board authorized the construction of some 'Pacific' locomotives with proportions generally similar to the 'XC' class, but with boilers carrying a pressure of 225 lb. per sq. in. instead of 180, and four cylinders instead of two. These locomotives were experimental in nature, and had camshaft-operated poppet valves. They were allocated to the heaviest main-line work of the North Western Railway, operating between Delhi and Peshawar, on the one hand, and on the other, between Lahore and Karachi. At the time of their introduction they were the heaviest and most powerful locomotives in Asia. They had four cylinders 16 in. diameter by 26 in. stroke; the coupled wheels were 6 ft. 2 in. diameter, and the tractive effort 34,400 lb. Full advantage was taken of the excellence of the permanent way, on the stretches of broad-gauge main line over which they operated, to use an axle-load of 21½ tons. The total weight of engine and tender in working order was 172 tons. These engines did some excellent work on the important mail trains.

86 Bengal Nagpur Railway: Four-cylinder de Glehn Compound 'Pacific'.

In the early 1900s the Bengal Nagpur Railway adopted the de Glehn compound system in a series of 'Atlantic' engines designed very much in the style of the famous four-cylinder compound 'Atlantics' on the Northern Railway of France. In the 1920s, with the outstanding success of the latest French 'Pacifics' in view, the Bengal Nagpur Railway placed an order with the North British Locomotive Company for some of the largest passenger locomotives that had then been seen in India. These were also de Glehn compounds, with the machinery arranged exactly as in the latest French examples, but as will be seen from our picture, the general appearance was essentially British. The high-pressure cylinders outside were 16½ in. diameter by 26 in. stroke, and the large low-pressure cylinders, inside, were 25 in. diameter. Full advantage was taken of the Indian standard gauge of 5 ft. 6 in. to make a spacious layout of the machinery inside. The boiler pressure was 250 lb. per sq. in. The engines were hand fired, with the reasonably good coal mined on the railway route. These large engines weighed 169½ tons, with their tenders, and the tractive effort was 28,700 lb.

87 London and North Eastern Railway: Thirsk New Signal Box.

Thirsk, brought into service in 1933, represented an entirely new conception in railway signalling operation. It was an all-power job, with searchlight-type colour-light signals, and all-electric point operation, but the novelty lay in the regulation of the traffic, not from a miniature lever interlocking frame but from a very small panel equipped with small thumb switches. These switches themselves were not interlocked. Any one of them could be turned at will; but the safety of the train movements through a junction, where there was perhaps more consistently fast running than anywhere else than in Great Britain, was ensured by interlocking between the various control circuits. If the signalman inadvertently turned a switch to make a movement that was then unsafe the electric circuit interlocking prevented any movement taking place. The outward effect of the new technique was to be seen in the shape of the signal box. The upper storey providing the panel, or operating, room was very small; but the ground floor was extensive, to house the considerable amount of electrical gear necessary to provide the circuit interlocking. In its broad principles, if not in detail, Thirsk was the prototype of all modern signalling development in Great Britain.

88 Newcastle Central: Old Signal Box.

The working of points and signals by means other than mechanical levers, rodding, and wires was introduced to a limited extent in Great Britain from the turn of the century. It lessened the signalman's work, and by the miniaturization of the interlocking lever frames and the concentration of control gave the men a better chance of supervising, by the routes they set up and the signals they cleared, the general flow of traffic. In those early days, however, power was used purely for actuation. The great science of track-circuit control had yet to come, and so it continued to be necessary for signalmen to see the trains. The innovation of the illuminated track diagram, whereby the whereabouts of trains on a layout could be indicated by lights had not yet been applied to main-line railways. The signal box at Newcastle shown in our picture is representative of the beginnings of our period, and of the kind of positioning that soon ceased to be necessary. This signal box was mounted on a gallery above the tracks so that the men could see all the train movements at one end of the station. Now no such vantage point is necessary; in fact, at Newcastle itself there was installed in the 1950s a new signal box from which the men do not see any trains at all. They work, and set up the routes required, entirely on the illuminated diagram indications.

89 **Great Western Railway:** Bristol Temple Meads East, Power Signal Box.

The signalling scheme brought into service during the 1930s reflected, in the signal-box architecture, the changing fashions in domestic and business-house architecture of the day. At the same time the fortress-like appearance was not by any means entirely a matter of style. Bristol was re-equipped with a modern system of electric power signalling, and the signal box itself had to house a large amount of intricate electrical apparatus. Furthermore, it was the tendency to concentrate much of the equipment previously contained in a multitude of lineside cases in the signal box itself, and run cable from the box to the outside functions. It may have been a little more expensive in cabling, but the convenience of having control apparatus concentrated in the signal box was a strong

argument for this change in practice. In addition to this, the likelihood of another Great War was becoming more than a vague possibility at that time, and new signal boxes were being built to more substantial proportions to minimize the risk of damage to electrical apparatus in air raids. For all these factors, as our picture shows, a very handsomely styled signal box was built, and it was still in service until the spring of 1970.

90 **Alsace-Lorraine Railways:** Mulhouse Signal Box.

The provinces of Alsace and Lorraine suffered to a considerable extent from the effects of International conflict. After the Franco-Prussian war of 1870–1 they were annexed by Germany, and the railways in those in those two former French provinces became unique among the railways of Germany. In the various states which formed the German Empire the administration of the railways was in local hands, and there were, for example, separate railway systems in Bavaria, Saxony, Wurtemberg, and on both sides of the Rhine. After 1871 the Alsace-Lorraine system was placed under the direct control of the Imperial Government, in Berlin, and all its equipment was thoroughly Germanized, including a change from left-hand to right-hand running. After the end of the First World War the two provinces were restored to France, though except in the case of new installations no move was made to replace, or alter, the German equipment. The fine new electrical plant at Mulhouse, of which we illustrate the handsome signal box, was entirely French, and the box itself represents an interesting variety in architecture to the British signal boxes in references 87 and 89.

91 **Malayan Railways:** Three-cylinder 'Pacific' Express Passenger Locomotive.

At the time these locomotives were introduced in 1938 the maximum axle load permitted on the main lines of the Malayan Railways was 12¾ tons. Yet on metre gauge track the loading of the mail trains between Singapore, Kuala Lumpur, and Prai was such as to require a powerful locomotive. On the part of the line ascending the Taiping Pass, near Ipoh, there are heavy gradients. The engine illustrated in our picture is a skilful design, providing a tractive effort of 22,130 lb. Very great care was taken to reduce weight whenever possible. Bar frames are used, and the boiler was kept relatively small by adopting a high steam pressure of 250 lb. per sq. in. and a shell built up from high-tensile nickel-steel plates. A smaller volume of steam, from a smaller boiler, but at high pressure, provided the necessary latent energy for developing a high tractive power. The three cylinders are 12½ in. diameter by 24 in. stroke, and the coupled wheels 4 ft. 6 in. diameter. In recent years new diesel–electric locomotives have been put on to the mail trains, and these excellent 4-6-2s are fully employed on freight.

92 **Royal State Railways of Thailand:** American-built Three-cylinder 'Pacific' Locomotive.

In Thailand, or Siam as the country was known when these locomotives were introduced, the lines of communication in the rich, rice-producing areas were very much dependent upon rail transport. Although connection with the Malayan railway was made at Padang Besar, at the southern extremity of the line, there was then little international traffic, and trade from north to south of the country flowed into and out of Bangkok. The railway is metre gauge, and laid with relatively light rail, on a somewhat spongy road bed—at any rate in the rice-growing and jungle country. Freight traffic is heavy, and powerful locomotives were needed, and to get the maximum power-weight ratio without the risk of incurring wheel-slip from a tractive effort high in relation to adhesion weight, the three-cylinder system of propulsion was adopted for new 'Pacific' and 2-8-2 engines purchased from the U.S.A. in 1925. One of the 'Pacifics' is illustrated in our picture. There were eventually 26 of these fine engines in service. Like the great majority of Thai locomotives, even today, they are wood fired. The tenders when fully stacked up carry enough logs of soft timber for a run of about 120 or 140 miles, according to the load being hauled, and the lengths of run are so arranged that an engine can travel out and back to its home station on one tenderful. The lengths of run are thus relatively short, with frequent engine changing *en route*.

93 **Malayan Railways:** Two-cylinder 4-6-4 Tank Engine.

Under reference 91 the new three-cylinder 'Pacific' locomotives for main-line working are described and illustrated. In addition to the long runs from Singapore to the frontier of Thailand, this railway has a number of branches where a tender engine is not ideal. In consequence, a tank engine version of this same design was prepared—similar in most respects, but not interchangeable so far as details were concerned. The most important difference was that the tank engines were two-cylinder only, having cylinders 14½ in. diameter by 22 in. stroke; coupled wheels 4 ft. 6 in. diameter, and the same high boiler pressure as the main-line 'Pacifics', 250 lb. per sq. in. The locomotive had a very light maximum axle-load with a total of only $37\frac{1}{4}$ tons on the three coupled axles. The all-up weight of the engine in working order was 74 tons. They were fitted with cow-catchers at both ends, rendering the locomotives suitable for service running in both directions and obviating any need for turning at the outer termini of branch lines, as for example, that from Kuala Lumpur to Port Swettenham. Like the main-line 'Pacifics', these 4-6-4 tank engines were fitted with the Caprotti valve gear.

94 Burma Railways: 2-6-4 Suburban Tank Locomotive.

In years between the two world wars the Burma Railways experienced a striking increase in local traffic around the Capital City of Rangoon, and in conformity with British practice of the day, this increased demand was met by the introduction of a modern design of tank engine. In contrast to earlier engines in the British tradition supplied to the countries of South-East Asia, the new engines, built by Robert Stephenson and Hawthorns Ltd., were designed for maximum accessibility of all parts needed attention: valve gear, piping, fittings, all were arranged outside, so that full servicing could be carried out without the need to get over a pit. The resulting locomotive was workmanlike and functional, rather than handsome; but admirably fulfilling the need of the day. The leading dimensions were cylinders 15 in. diameter by 22 in. stroke; coupled-wheel diameter 3 ft. 7 in.; a boiler pressure of 180 lb. per sq. in. The total weight on the three coupled axles was only $28\frac{3}{4}$ tons, and the complete locomotive, in working order, weighed only $55\frac{3}{4}$ tons. The boiler was small, with a grate area of only $12\frac{3}{4}$ sq. ft., while the tractive effort was 17,613 lb.

95 London, Midland and Scottish Railway: The Stanier 'Black Five' Mixed Traffic 4-6-0.

The second outcome of the L.M.S.R. 'scrap and build' policy of the 1930s (see ref. 96) was the celebrated 'Black Five' 4-6-0, officially known as the '5P5F' class. It is no exaggeration to state that this class, which eventually numbered 855 engines, was one of the most generally useful types of steam locomotive to run in any country the world over. They were light on maintenance, moderate in coal consumption, most reliable and at their best could be extended to such an extent as to deputize for the largest 'Pacific' engines. They worked anywhere on the L.M.S.R. system: from London to Wick, to Kyle of Lochalsh, to Hull, to Swansea, over the Somerset and Dorset line to Bournemouth, while after nationalization their spheres of activity were extended to the West Highland line in Scotland, and to certain duties over the North to West route from Shrewsbury to Hereford. They would run freely up to 90 m.p.h. with express trains on the Midland lines, and seemed just as much at home slogging it out with a heavy freight train. Our picture shows one of the earliest engines of the class fitted with domeless boiler. Later varieties had domed boilers and a higher degree of superheat, though the performance of all varieties was highly satisfactory. Their leading dimensions were: cylinders $18\frac{1}{2}$ in. diameter by 28 in. stroke; coupled wheels 6 ft. 0 in. diameter; grate area 28.65 sq. ft.; boiler pressure 225 lb. per sq. in.; tractive effort 25,455 lb.

96 **London, Midland and Scottish Railway:** The '5XP' 'Jubilee' Class 4-6-0.

In the 1930s large-scale standardization of motive power was in progress on the L.M.S.R. The Chief Mechanical Engineer, W. A. Stanier, had received authority for a policy of 'scrap and build'. It was considered that the replacement of large numbers of medium-powered locomotives from the constituent companies, of a diversity of designs, by new standard engines would enable the traffic to be worked with fewer individual engines, and the programme of repair and maintenance work would be simplified. Stanier responded to this mandate with the 'Jubilee' class of three-cylinder 4-6-0, for intermediate express duty; a class that was used all over the former Midland Railway, on cross-country services over the Lancashire and Yorkshire line, and on all routes in Scotland except those in the Highlands. No fewer than 190 of these engines were built, and they proved hard working, free steaming, and very speedy machines. They were just as at home in fast lightly loaded duties, as in slogging up the heavy inclines of the Scottish lines between Glasgow and Carlisle. They were all named, in a diversity of titles that recalled the days of the London and North Western Railway.

97 **Paris, Lyons, and Mediterranean Railway:** Four-cylinder Compound 'Pacific'.

The 'PLM', to use the well-known abbreviation for the title of this great railway, had some distinctly different operating conditions to work with on the succeeding sections of its long main line from Paris to the Côte d'Azur. Under reference 21 there is described and illustrated the huge 4-8-2 type of locomotive designed for the mountain section between Laroche and Dijon. Elsewhere, between Paris and Marseilles, the line was remarkably level, and engines of the Pacific type were used right down to the time of electrification. The 'PLM' developed the compound 'Pacific' to a very high degree of efficiency, and our picture shows one of the Series 'D' engines, which by the year 1930 had numerous aids to free running and low fuel consumption. The 'PLM' Pacifics were the last to remain in regular express passenger working in France, and as the electrification of their own line extended a number of 'PLM' engines were transferred to both the Eastern and Northern lines. Until the year 1968 they worked between Calais and Amiens, having superseded the Northern Railway's own Pacifics of the Collin type (ref. 2), and worked alongside the famous Chapelon Pacifics of the P.O. Midi (ref. 44).

98 **Netherlands State Railways:** 4-8-4 Tank Engine.

The Dutch railways used four-cylinder propulsion for most of their 4-6-0 passenger locomotives, and when the time came for introduction of new engines for the heavy coal traffic in the Limburg district the authorities specified a four-cylinder single-expansion tank engine of the 4-8-4 type, having many parts standard with the four-cylinder 4-6-0 express locomotives. In earlier years the Dutch had purchased largely from England, and from Beyer Peacock in particular, and although these new 4-8-4 engines were built in Germany, by Henschel & Sohn, of Kassel, they had a remarkably British appearance, in their neatness of outline, absence of externally mounted fittings, and in the ornate finish, with copper-capped chimney, and polished brass dome cover. They were powerful engines. The four cylinders were 16½ in. diameter by 26 in. stroke; coupled-wheel diameter 5 ft. 1 in., and the boiler had an evaporative heating surface of 1796 sq. ft. and a superheating surface of 538 sq. ft. The grate area was 34 sq. ft. The total weight of engine in working order was 124½ tons, making them among the heaviest tank engines then operating in Europe. The tractive effort was 32,413 lb. For a heavy, short-haul, coal engine this was certainly a very handsome design.

99 **South Australian Railways:** The '520' Class Lightweight 4-8-4.

This striking looking locomotive belongs to the very end of our period, design-wise; and because of war conditions the first examples were not completed at the Islington Works of the South Australian Railways till 1944. They were designed to work on routes laid with rails weighing only 60 lb. to the yard, and although looking so huge and impressive, were really a moderate-sized locomotive, weighing only 104 tons, without tender. The 4-8-4 wheel arrangement had to be used to secure the requisite adhesion weight, and this made the engine in-ordinately long. The boiler is, however, not nearly so long as it appears. If it had been, the heating surface would have been considerably in excess of requirements and the engine too heavy. Some clever design work was involved in keeping the weight and maintaining an impressive appearance. The cylinders were 20½ in. diameter by 28 in. stroke; coupled-wheel diameter

5 ft. 6 in., and the boiler had 2451 sq. ft. of evaporative heating surface and 651 sq. ft. of superheater. The grate area was 45 sq. ft. The maximum axle load was skilfully kept down to no more than 15 tons. These engines operated on 5 ft. 3 in. gauge lines.

100 **Victorian Railways:** Class 'X' 2-8-2 Goods Locomotive.

At the turn of the century the Victorian Railways were perhaps the most 'English' of all the Australian railways, so far as locomotive designs were concerned. Neat and compact outlines, gay liveries well embellished with polished brass and copper, handsomely styled chimneys distinguished passenger and goods engines alike. By the end of the First World War things had become much more functional. Plain stove-pipe chimneys came into vogue; the livery, even for express pas-senger engines, became plain black, and running plates were raised to expose the full extent of the wheels and give ready access to the valve gear, for which outside Walschaerts was taking the place of Stephenson's link motion, inside. Our picture, showing the 'X' class 2-8-2 goods engine of 1929, illustrates the evolution of this line of transition, and to a plain, austere outline were added the gaunt accessories of smoke-deflecting plates. These followed the practice currently being adopted on the continent of Europe and in Great Britain, in carrying these up-ward and continuously from the running plate. It was later found that while the upward extent was necessary, it was not of any advantage to carry them down-wards much below the centre line of the boiler. They were cut off accordingly, and looked even more horrible!

101 **Victorian Railways:** Class 'S' 4-6-2 Express Passenger Locomotive.

Despite the trend towards austerity in appearance evidenced by the 2-8-2 freight engine (ref. 100), when it came to the development of a new express passenger design much of the old artistry returned, though not to the extent of putting the engines into a coloured livery. Plain black remained in fashion, though when the outline is as graceful as in the 'S' class engines of 1928, colour is a lesser consideration. The Victorian Railways, like their neighbours in South Australia, use the 5 ft. 3 in. gauge. In working the Inter-State Expresses at the period under review through trains could be run between Melbourne and Adelaide, but northwards to Sydney the Victorian locomotives and stock could work only as far as the State boundary. There passengers had to change into the 4 ft. 8½ in. gauge trains of New South Wales. The 'S' class engines worked the principal express trains on both these interstate routes, and when the celebrated 'Spirit of Progress' train was introduced in 1937 for the Melbourne–Sydney service some engines of the 'S' class were streamlined, in the prevailing fashion. This, of course, obscured their handsome lines, which are well brought out in our picture.

102 **Western Australian Government Railways:** 'Pacific' Type Express Goods Locomotive Class 'PR'.

In 1924 this railway took delivery from the North British Locomotive Company of ten 4-6-2 engines for fast goods and general service. They were designated Class 'P', and a further fifteen were built in the Western Australian Government Railways workshops at Midland. These engines gave a good account of themselves, but in 1938 greater power was needed on this 3 ft. 6 in. gauge system, and the Class 'P' was redesigned to have a higher boiler pressure and greater adhesion weight. As such they became very useful engines, capable of taking a freight train load of 555 tons on a 1 in 80 gradient. For a British-built engine they have a distinctly American appearance, except for the shapely chimney. Seventeen of these engines are now in service, and in their rebuilt condition, known as Class 'PR', they have been dignified by the addition of names—all of Western Australian rivers. As rebuilt they have two cylinders 19 in. diameter by 26 in. stroke; coupled wheels 4 ft. 6 in. diameter; a boiler having an evaporative heating surface of 1494 sq. ft., and a superheating surface of 354 sq. ft. The grate area is 35 sq. ft. The total weight in working order is 102½ tons, and the tractive effort 25,855 lb.

103 **Great Western Railway:** The Pioneer Diesel Mechanical Railcar.

In earlier years the Great Western had been one of the largest users of steam rail motor cars, but in the early 1930s there began a remarkable development in the use of diesel power. One of the principal criticisms of the old steam units had been their slowness. No such criticism was expected from the diesel cars, which were designed to run at 70 m.p.h. or more. Working with the Associated Equipment Company, of Southall, builders of the London buses, a lightweight, partially streamlined unit was introduced in 1934, which immediately became very popular with travellers. The drive was entirely mechanical through a standard gearbox, and many are the amusing tales told of steam-locomotive drivers learning how to change gear. At that time few members of the artisan class in Great Britain owned motor cars, and the technique of driving was a novelty. Some felt it was a trifle *infra-dig*, and one driver, after a day's struggling with the gears, confessed that he hardly dared to go home 'and tell the missus he'd been driving a motor bus'! Many more larger and still faster cars were put on to the line, and they did an enormous amount of very useful work.

104 Turkish State Railways: Steam Railcar.

Steam rail motor cars were very popular on the railways of Great Britain in the 1900–20 period, though in the years between the two world wars their use was declining, and the introduction of diesel cars had begun. One of the disadvantages found in Great Britain was that the whole unit could be out of action if the engine portion needed attention. This contingency is ingeniously provided for in the Turkish car illustrated, which was one of a number built by the Esslingen Company, of Stuttgart. These cars have the power bogie as a complete unit in itself, and when uncoupled could be used as an auxiliary locomotive, or could be replaced by another when repairs were necessary. The passenger saloon was spacious, and had accommodation for first-, second-, and third-class passengers. The maximum speed of the car in normal service was 75 km. per hour (46½ m.p.h.), but on trial speeds up to 67 m.p.h. were attained on level track. The unit had remarkable hill-climbing abilities. On a gradient of 1 in 70 a speed of 50 m.p.h. was sustained, while in real mountain conditions, on a gradient of 1 in 44 with many severe curves, a speed of 37 m.p.h. was easily sustained.

105 London and North Eastern Railway: 'Clayton'-type Steam Railcar.

During the 1900–10 period when the steam railcar became popular on the railways of Britain, small steam locomotives of orthodox type were used as motive power. Their introduction met with varying degrees of success, and although some units, such as those of the Great Western and of the Lancashire and Yorkshire Railway, put in many years of hard working, there was no technical development until the early 1920s, when the development of a high-speed geared engine with a high-pressure water-tube boiler opened up new possibilities. The L.N.E.R., under Sir Nigel Gresley, was, however, the only British railway to use the new technique to any extent, and our picture illustrates one of the first, built by the Clayton Wagon Company of Lincoln in 1928. These handsome little cars all had names of famous stage coaches. The eleven Clayton cars did not have a long life, but a modified form introduced by the Sentinel Wagon Works, in conjunction with Cammell Laird, had greater success. There were two varieties, one with a chain drive, and the other gear drive. At one time there were no less than 73 of them in service on the L.N.E.R.

106 German Federal Railways: The 'Glass' Car Working Tours from Munich.

Although primarily a book about steam trains in the period under review, one cannot be other than mindful of the encroachment of newer forms of railway traction, and among a group of railcars that includes at least one diesel it is certainly permissible to add this very attractive electrically propelled car. It was built in 1935, and used for advertised and private-hire tours over some of the most picturesque mountain sections of the German railways and regularly penetrated as far into Austria as Innsbruck. This beautiful car seats 72 passengers on swing-over seats, and is entirely glass above the waistline. This makes it particularly attractive on sightseeing runs, over routes where the mountains often tower almost vertically above the railway. More than this there are two opening panels, one at each end, for travelling in fine weather. Its maximum speed is 68 m.p.h. When first built it was finished in an all-cream livery, but we have chosen to depict it in the present style of red and cream. Easily the most spectacular run made by the 'Glass' car is from Munich via Garmisch, over the mountain summit at Seefeld to Hochzirl, and then down an almost frightening descent into the upper Inn valley, and so to Innsbruck.

107 Atchison, Topeka, and Santa Fé Railroad: The '3771' Class 4–8–4.

These magnificent locomotives, built by the Baldwin Locomotive Company in 1938, are among the most remarkable that have ever run the road anywhere in the world. They were essentially high-speed express passenger machines and used to work such celebrated trains as 'The Chief' and 'The Fast Mail' throughout between Kansas City and Los Angeles, a distance of 1488 miles. During this run they would be handled, in succession, by nine different crews. Their merit lay in an ability to stand 'all-out' thrashing up the many severe gradients, and then to be run just as hard downhill or on the level at 90–100 m.p.h. They were oil-fired and operated on the minimum of servicing. After the twenty-six-hour run from Kansas City to Los Angeles no more than three hours

turn-round time was necessary before returning on an equally hard eastbound assignment. The two cylinders were 28 in. diameter by 32 in. stroke; boilers had 5313 sq. ft. evaporative heating surface, 2366 sq. ft. superheating surface, and 108 sq. ft. grate area. The boiler pressure was 300 lb. per sq. in., and this in combination with 6 ft. 8 in. diameter driving wheels gave a tractive effort of 66,000 lb. The total weight of engine and tender in working order was 427 tons.

108 Union Pacific Railroad: Three-cylinder 4–12–2 Heavy Freight Engine.

The Union Pacific takes a more northerly route through the Rocky Mountains than the Denver and Rio Grande, and has the advantage of rather easier gradients, and rather less in the way of curvature. Even so, the term 'easier' is used only in a relative sense, and its enormous freight trains demanded very hard locomotive work. At a time when the whole trend of American locomotive practice was towards the simplest possible layout of machinery the Union Pacific applied the three-cylinder principle, with which the builders, the American Locomotive Company, had wide experience in construction of 4–10–2 engines for the Southern Pacific. To avoid having any inside motion work, the Gresley conjugated type of gear was used, as on the London and North Eastern Railway. These enormous rigid-wheelbase engines were originally limited to 35 m.p.h.; but their riding was so steady that speeds up to 60 m.p.h. were afterwards permitted. The boilers were of much the same proportions as the Santa Fé '3771', but with lower boiler pressure, of 220 lb. per sq. in. The tractive effort was 96,600 lb. and the total weight in working order 350 tons. Between 1926 and 1930 no fewer than ninety of these engines were built by ALCO for the Union Pacific Railroad.

109 London and North Eastern Railway: The 'Royal Train' 4-4-0 (London–Wolferton).

The Royal country residence at Sandringham, Norfolk, was served by the small station of Wolferton, on the line from Kings Lynn to Hunstanton, and to provide for occasional Royal Train journeys to and from London two locomotives stationed at Kings Lynn were maintained in specially good condition. For these short, daytime journeys a relatively short train was needed, and two standard express passenger 4-4-0s of the former Great Eastern 'Claud Hamilton' class were used. Ordinarily they worked in the regular passenger link; but whereas engines in this class and power classification were painted black, the two engines earmarked for Royal Train workings were finished in the apple-green style of the first-line express engines. Moreover, all the brass and copper work was kept highly burnished; the buffers and side rods were polished, and even when engaged on ordinary passenger duties these two engines 8783 and 8787 were superbly turned out. The crews and shed staff at Kings Lynn took an immense pride in them, and no special preparation or cleaning up was needed if a Royal Train was required at relatively short notice.

110 London, Midland and Scottish Railway: The Record-breaking Stanier 'Pacific' Princess Elizabeth.

In 1933 the first two 'Pacific' engines for the L.M.S.R. were completed at Crewe Works. These two engines were experimental, in their sheer size, and in the many innovations in construction. For the first time also they made possible a through locomotive working over the 401 miles between London and Glasgow. Although doing much good work, they were, at first, not entirely satisfactory; but the experience thus gained was put to excellent use, and from 1935 onwards, when further engines of the same general type were built with certain modifications in design their performance became superb. Our picture shows one of the most famous of the class, No. 6201 Princess Elizabeth; this engine, in November 1936, made two record non-stop runs between London and Glasgow, northbound in 353¾ minutes with a load of 225 tons, and southbound on the following day in 344¼ minutes with 260 tons—the latter an average of exactly 70 m.p.h. These are still the fastest runs ever made with any form of rail traction between the two cities.

111 South African Railways: The '15CA' 4-8-2 Mixed Traffic Locomotive.

This remarkable-looking engine was one of the earlier products of the 'big-engine' era in South Africa. At one time it seemed as though the railway administration would accept the exigencies of the 3 ft. 6 in. gauge and retain a 'narrow-gauge' outlook. But the loading gauge permitted the use of locomotives that were as tall as those on the British home railways, and much wider. From that time onwards, with suitable strengthening of the track, very large engines were introduced on which the only sub-standard dimension was the rail gauge itself. The '15CA' was introduced in 1926 for main-line passenger and freight working on the mountain sections. They are two-cylinder simples with 23 in. by 28 in. cylinders, 4 ft. 9 in. coupled wheels, and a total weight, engine and tender in working order, of 170 tons. The tractive effort of the earlier batches, with 23-in.-diameter cylinders, is 38,980 lb., but in later batches the enormous boiler was found capable of supplying still larger cylinders and the diameter was increased to 24 in., bringing the tractive effort up to 42,440 lb. All these engines are still in service, though superseded on the heaviest 4–8–2 duties by the still larger and more powerful '15F' class.

112 **Chinese National Railways:** Canton–Hankow Line. 4–8–4 Mixed Traffic Locomotive of 1934.

These imposing and very efficient locomotives are undoubtedly among the most remarkable ever exported from Great Britain. They were designed under the direction of Col. K. Cantlie, mechanical engineering adviser to the Chinese Government of the day, and built by the Vulcan Foundry Co. Ltd. They were designed for heavy passenger and freight service, and to work over the northern section of the line, negotiating gradients of 1 in 70 and much sharp curvature. At the same time other engines of the same class were required for fast running over the level stretches of the Shanghai–Nanking line. Both classes of duty had in common the need to burn low-grade coal. The success of these engines may be judged from the fact that all twenty-four of them are still in service today, nearly thirty years after their first introduction. The cylinders are $20\frac{7}{8}$ in. diameter by $29\frac{1}{2}$ in. stroke; coupled wheel diameter is 5 ft. 9 in.; and boiler pressure 220 lb. per sq. in. The tractive effort is 32,920 lb. The tenders are enormous, having a capacity for 6600 gallons of water and $11\frac{3}{4}$ tons of coal. With a huge fire grate area of 67·8 sq. ft. and poor-quality coal, a mechanical stoker was essential. Six of these engines, allocated

to the steep northern section of the Canton–Hankow line, had booster-driven bogies on their tenders.

113 **Soviet Russian Railways:** The Standard 'SU' Class 2–6–2 of 1932, 5 ft. Gauge.

From the year 1924 there was a need for a more powerful general-service locomotive that could be used on lines all over the U.S.S.R., and a new design of 2–6–2 was worked out, and first put into traffic in 1925. Quantity production was commenced at once, and several hundreds were built, and then in 1932 a slightly modified design was prepared, and this is the subject of our picture. These engines, like the initial 'batch' of 1925, and two subsequent 'batches' have two cylinders $22\frac{1}{2}$ in. diameter by $27\frac{1}{2}$ in. stroke, coupled wheels 6 ft. 1 in. diameter, a boiler pressure of 185 lb. per sq. in., and a tractive effort of 30,100 lb. With a maximum axle-load of no more than 18 tons they have a very high route availability. The word 'batch' is used in no more than a relative sense, because of the second, or 1932, 'batch' about 1000 engines were built, and of a further development before the Second World War, the third 'batch' 500 were built. There were therefore upwards of 2000 of the generally useful engines in service by 1939, and still further examples were built from 1947 onwards.

114 **Italian State Railways:** Four-cylinder 2–6–2 Express Locomotive.

The amalgamation of the various independent Italian railways into one nationally owned system led to the elimination of many curious earlier designs, such as the Planchard 0–6–4 express engines, and the two-cylinder compounds on the Mediterranean line. A new series of standard designs was evolved, having what could be termed a 'new look' and remarkable uniformity of style. In contrast to the styles of some Continental railways, the appearance was notably 'clean' and free from external gadgets hung on outside. The 2–6–2 forming the subject of our picture is a typical example. At the same time a distinguished Italian engineer, Arturo Caprotti, invented a new type of valve gear using poppet, rather than piston or slide, valves. It was not unlike the valves of an automobile. This proved very successful in giving a good distribution of steam, and a free exhaust; and many Italian locomotives, including that in our picture, had the Caprotti valve gear. It was adopted also to a limited extent in Great Britain, and in certain countries of the British Commonwealth, such as Malaya. The engine illustrated is a four-cylinder simple—a form much favoured in the later days of steam in Italy.

115 Madrid, Zaragoza and Alicante Railway: Mixed Traffic 4–8–0 Locomotive.

The M.Z.A. was an early user of the 4–8–0 type of locomotive, and derived much success from a number of units of this type purchased from Henschel. In 1920 an enlarged and improved design was worked out, and between that year and 1931 sixty-five of the new engines were built, all by Maquinista of Barcelona. They are extremely robust and powerful engines, and at the present time a number of them are oil-fired. Our picture shows one of the 2396–2420 batch of 1930. The building of all the engines of this class by the same contractor was unusual, in Spain. Today, apart from the former Norte and Central Aragon lines, they can be seen

working over a wide area of the R.E.N.F.E. system. Their principal dimensions are: cylinders $24\frac{1}{2}$ in. diameter by 26 in. stroke; coupled-wheel diameter 5 ft. 3 in., and total weight of engine and tender in working order 144 tons. The entire class is still in service.

116 Finnish State Railways: 2–8–2 Class Tr 1 Freight Locomotive.

The Finnish State Railways, radiating from the Capital City and headquarters at Helsinki, are laid to the same gauge, 5 ft. 0 in., as the Soviet Russian railways, which they link up with at the frontier roughly 100 miles from Leningrad. They have a route mileage of some 3200 miles, but as is to be expected, the traffic is not very intense, and it was operated by less than 800 locomotives. Recently a number of diesel-powered four-car train sets have been introduced, but much reliance is still placed on steam locomotives. For passenger work a class of Pacifics, known as Class Hr 1, handles the principal trains, but for our picture the Tr 1 2–8–2 engine has been chosen. These locomotives, because of their relatively high tractive power, are also called upon for passenger working of a heavy intermediate character. Their appearance suggests a likeness to contemporary Swedish designs of the 1930s. Interesting features are the bell, in the American style, carried on the top of the boiler and the generally neat outline. They would have been even more handsome had not the sandbox been combined with the steam-dome casing.

117 New York, New Haven and Hartford: Dining Car for the 'Yankee Clipper' Service.

The 'Yankee Clipper' and the 'Merchants Limited' were the names given to de luxe trains introduced in 1930 on the Shore Line between New York and Boston. Each train consisted of seven cars, including parlour, club, and observation saloons, and each train included one dining car. The 'Yankee Clipper' service provided departures from both cities at 3.30 p.m. and an arrival at 8.15 p.m. The dining cars, one of which is shown in our picture, made something of railway rolling-stock history by having mechanical refrigeration. Although so very plain externally, the dining saloons were beautifully appointed internally in the style of the so-called colonial design. Each car was named after a clipper ship which was well known in the days when much of the ocean-going commerce of New England was carried in sailing vessels. The windows were of nautical design in appearance, and in each car a reproduction of an original painting of the ship after which the car was named was hung on the end wall near the entrance. Technically the cars were of the usual massive American construction of the day, 80 ft. 5 in. long, and with high clerestory roofs. The latter, however, did not include any actual windows, only ventilating gear.

118 **Western Australian Government Railways:** Sleeping Car for the 'Westland' Express.

This fine vehicle strictly belongs to a period later than that of our book, being built in 1947, but it also now represents a past era. The rail gauge in Western Australia is 3 ft. 6 in. and until quite recently this involved a change of train at Kalgoorlie, where connection was made, in the Trans-Australian railway service, with the 4 ft. 8½ in. gauge trains of the Commonwealth system. Recently, however, an entirely new main line has been laid between

Kalgoorlie and Perth, so that the 4 ft. 8½ in. gauge trains now work through. The 'Westland' cars, although running on the 3 ft. 6 in., are most spacious. They contain eight two-berth cabins, with large personal wardrobes, electric fans, refrigerated drinking water, automatic ceiling ventilation, and they were the first railway coaches in Australia to have constant hot and cold water installed at the shower bath and in the wash-basins. The journey between Kalgoorlie and Perth on the 3 ft. 6 in. gauge took about 12 hours, and the cars were fitted with every amenity for travel in the extremes of climate experienced at different seasons in this part of Australia. The berths can readily be adapted for day use, and when so arranged provide seating for 24 passengers.

119 **Chicago, Milwaukee, St Paul and Pacific:** Super-dome Car.

'The Milwaukee Road', to give it the familiar title, was one of the earliest railways in the U.S.A. to introduce what may be termed 'fancy' trains. Under reference 146 will be found a description of the first locomotives built for the streamlined 'Hiawatha' express, and for the Milwaukee it was not enough merely to introduce stream-lining. It must be accompanied by gay colours to draw immediate and striking attention to the star trains. It was perhaps fitting that the Milwaukee should thus have been pioneer; for it was a pioneer in railroading west of Chicago. It was the first railway to be built in the State of Wisconsin, and it was the first to provide a railway service between Chicago and Minneapolis. That service later became highly competitive, and it was to keep in the forefront that the Milwaukee introduced the streamlined 'Hiawatha'. Dome cars were an innovation on scenic routes, and provided a fascinating novelty in first-class travel. The super-dome car illustrated provides accommodation for sixty-eight passengers in the observation dome, plus twenty-eight in the lounge below. In addition to its ultra-high-speed services, the Milwaukee extends through to the Pacific Coast to terminals at Seattle and Tacoma.

120 **French National Railways:** Third-class Corridor Carriage.

On the continent of Europe the period of this book opened with a large amount of wooden rolling stock still in use. Much of this had wooden underframing; its condition had not improved through the exigencies of war-time conditions, and when faulty operation or indifferent permanent way led to accidents in the first few post-war years the wooden coaches suffered severely, especially if they were marshalled in between modern all-steel stock. The wave of reaction from this situation was the building of much heavy all-steel stock, with tare weights of between 45 and 52 tons, in contrast to contemporary British coaches of 30–35 tons. The coach illustrated, however, represents a remarkable development of more modern times, in which welded construction and the use of lightweight materials has produced a coach seating 80 third-class passengers for a tare weight of 36 tons. These statistics are particularly interesting in the almost precise parallel they afford to the Great Western coaches of 1923 (ref. 11), which also seated 80 third-class passengers for a tare weight of 37 tons. The end construction of the French car will be noted, how the encircling shrouds encase the corridor connections and buffer against the adjoining coach.

121 **Buenos Aires Great Southern Railway:** Class '11C' 4–8–0 Heavy Goods Engine (Oil Fired).

This very powerful and successful design was introduced in 1924, and had a widely publicized début. The first 25 were built by Armstrong Whitworth and Co., and that firm included one of these engines on their stand at the British Empire Exhibition at Wembley in 1924. These engines had three cylinders, with three separate sets of Walschaerts valve gear, and were among the heaviest and most powerful goods engines ever put on the rail in Argentina. In 1929 a further 50 were supplied from England, 30 from Armstrong Whitworth and 20 from Beyer-Peacock. The three cylinders were $17\frac{1}{2}$ in. diameter by 26 in. stroke; coupled-wheel diameter 4 ft. $7\frac{1}{2}$ in. and boiler pressure 200 lb. per sq. in. The engine alone weighed 84 tons in working order. Much of the country traversed by the B.A.G.S. Railway involved haulage of freight trains of 1500–2000 tons, as well as the special seasonal express fruit trains from the Rio Negro valley into Buenos Aires. Although a number of diesel locomotives have subsequently been introduced in Argentina, all 75 of these fine engines are still in traffic.

122 **Buenos Aires Great Southern Railway:** The '12G' Class Three-cylinder 'Pacific'.

In the 1920s the B.A.G.S. Railway seemed fairly wedded to three-cylinder propulsion, though unlike the British L.N.E.R., the conjugated form of valve gear was not used. In 1927–8 the Vulcan Foundry of Newton-le-Willows, Lancashire, built 20 very fine 'Pacific' engines for high-speed work, and they had the large coupled-wheel diameter of 6 ft. 6 in.

They were an immediate success, and proved themselves easily master of any express passenger job to which they would be assigned. As originally built they had the unusual feature of having the two outside cylinders larger than the one inside cylinder, 19 in. diameter, against $17\frac{1}{2}$ in. This arose out of a fear that the heavy thrust from the inside cylinder might give rise to fractures of the crankshaft. In service they proved remarkably free from trouble, however, and by their light maintenance charges were as popular with the shed and management staff as they were with the footplate men. In 1931 an additional engine was built specially by the Vulcan Foundry for exhibition at the British Trade Fair held in Buenos Aires that year. Subsequently various slight modifications have been made, but all 21 engines were still in traffic at the end of 1967.

123 Buenos Aires Pacific Railway: 2–8–2 Mixed Traffic Locomotive.

The broad-gauge main lines of the Argentine, with a gauge of 5 ft. 6 in. were mostly heavily laid and capable of bearing large axle-loads. On most of the lines radiating from Buenos Aires the first stretches were reasonably level, and this encouraged the traffic departments to work extremely heavy trains. On the B.A.P.R. an axle load of $21\frac{1}{2}$ tons was permitted, and in 1928 Messrs. Beyer, Peacock and Co. built the very fine 2–8–2 engines illustrated, having a total weight with tender, of no less than 205 tons in working order. They are very simple, straightforward yet powerful engines having two cylinders $24\frac{1}{2}$ in. diameter by 30 in. stroke; coupled wheels 5 ft. 7 in. diameter, and with a boiler pressure of 200 lb. per sq. in. the tractive effort is no less than 40,290 lb. The tenders are

very large, having a capacity of 7700 gallons of water and 15 tons of coal. These tenders provided what is believed to be the first example, on a British-built locomotive, of a steam-operated coal pusher, by which the fireman can get coal forward at later stages in a long run without incurring the labour of climbing up into the tender and shovelling it forward.

124 Buenos Aires Great Southern Railway: The '12H' Class 4–6–0.

The level character of the principal main lines of this railway, and the absence of any very fast schedules, enabled the locomotives for both passenger and freight work to be comparatively small. Although certain 'Pacifics' had been introduced, by the mid-1930s reliance was still being placed upon 4–6–0s for the bulk of the main-line passenger work. The locomotive illustrated, one of a class of nine put into traffic in 1938, is interesting in that only the chassis and boiler was purchased from England. The engines were designed, and eventually erected, at the Liniers Works of the Buenos Aires Western Railway, which at that time came under the same management as the B.A.G.S. Railway. They had two cylinders, 19 in. diameter by 28 in. stroke; coupled wheels 6 ft. diameter, and a short, large-diameter boiler, and a firebox having a grate area of 25 sq. ft. Like most B.A.G.S. locomotives, they are oil-fired. All are still in service today, and bear names of former Argentine presidents and other political personalities. They have done good work with main-line passenger trains of an intermediate character.

125 London, Midland and Scottish Railway: 20-ton Hopper Wagon.

One of the problems in British railway operating lies in the restrictions in space imposed by the early pioneering conditions, which became so encompassed with other establishments alongside the railway that it would have been extremely expensive to make changes. In consequence, the four-wheeled wagon with a maximum capacity of about 20 tons remained the British standard. One can compare, perhaps with a little envy, the smart L.M.S.R. hopper wagon illustrated with the gigantic Pennsylvania vehicle (ref. 60) designed to carry 76 tons of coal. The L.M.S.R. wagons, of which 400 were put into service in 1930, were of all-steel construction, and designed for working in loose-coupled unbraked trains. An independent double brake was fitted on both sides, operated by a hand lever at diagonal left-hand corners. When descending very severe gradients a stop was made at the summit to enable the guard to pin down the hand brakes on a specified number of vehicles. The hopper doors were operated by hand, by an ingenious mechanism that enabled the load to be discharged with a minimum of physical effort to the man concerned. These wagons were used principally for the conveyance of iron ore.

126 **Great Western Railway:** 10-ton Fish Van 'Bloater'.

For obvious reasons fish is always a priority traffic on railways, and the special trains in connection with the major fishery seasons are run at speeds very little below those of express passenger trains. In the case of smaller consignments a number of vans are sometimes attached to passenger trains. Although the vans are fitted with continuous automatic brakes and screw couplings, one could not expect a four-wheeled wagon to run safely at the highest express train speeds, and on the

Great Western Railway certain express passenger trains on most routes were timed to schedules on which speeds much in excess of 60 m.p.h. were not required, and these were earmarked as suitable for the attaching of four-wheeled wagons. The vehicle shown in our picture is a good example of a specialized Great Western design, with a relatively long wheelbase, and a tare weight of 11 tons, for a 10-ton pay load. The name BLOATER is a code word specifying the type of vehicle and is referred to in railway operating telegrams. All special GWR vehicles had such names: GRANO signified a covered hopper wagon for grain; MOGO was an open truck, and perhaps a little inappropriate DOGFISH was a hopper wagon carrying ballast for the permanent way.

127 **Belgian National Railways:** Refrigerator Van for International Traffic.

One cannot travel far on the continent of Europe without seeing many long-wheelbased refrigerator vans, with their characteristic top ventilators revolving rapidly. These vehicles are in general use in Western Europe for Interfrigo traffic, but for operating purposes are based with various of the railways. The particular example which forms the subject of our picture is based at Antwerp, Belgian National Railways. These vehicles are designed for fast running. The long wheelbase gives steadiness of riding, and roller bearings provide freedom from incidental heating troubles. Express freight trains are not, of course, run at the speed of Trans-European Expresses, but normally sustain speeds of around 100 km. per hour (62 m.p.h.). On the critical sections through the Alps, such as the Gotthard and Lötschberg routes, there is no difference between passenger and freight train speeds. All are run at the maximum permitted by the physical characteristics of the line, and this enables the line to be used to its maximum advantage. These long-wheelbased Continental freight vehicles are remarkably steady in action. Even when running at maximum speed there is an absence of the nosing and hunting that one often sees with four-wheeled wagons.

128 German State Railways: All-welded 20-ton Freight Wagon.

Reference has already been made in this volume (refs. 12 and 13) to the efforts being made to reduce the dead weight of passenger stock on the continent of Europe. The present illustration shows one example of the similar drive to reduce weight in freight wagons. Generally speaking, Continental freight wagons are much larger than their British contemporaries, though the vehicle illustrated is not a particularly large one. The weight reduction effected was of the order of 10 per cent. Prior to the introduction of welding, Continental wagons had been generally of steel construction, though this was not the case in Great Britain. Indeed, there was considerable opposition to the use of all-steel wagons in favour of the old traditional design with wooden bodies. Ultimately, of course, the growing scarcity of suitable timber and its increasing price forced the issue. In Germany the practice of building steel wagons by welding methods began in 1927, in the construction of some large tank wagons which had not only to have the requisite strength but which were also to be liquid-tight at the joints. The successful outcome of this first essay began the chain of very advantageous development.

129 Canadian Pacific Railway: The 'Royal Hudson' Class 4-6-4.

It is perhaps appropriate to commence this quartet of Canadian engines with the 'Royal Hudsons', although this was the most recent of the designs. It was a development of the '2800' Hudson (ref. 132), and received its special title through engine No. 2850 of this class being specially selected to work the Royal Train when their Majesties King George VI and Queen Elizabeth toured Canada in 1939. 'Hudson' is the class name for the 4-6-4, just as 'Pacific' denotes the 4-6-2, and 'Atlantic' the 4-4-2. In Europe, however, the 4-6-4 type is known as the 'Baltic'. The 'Hudson' class, of which 30 were built in 1937, and were numbered from 2820 onwards, differed from their progenitors of 1929 by having domeless boilers, and a degree of streamlining. The Royal engine, No. 2850, was specially prepared and had a coronet on the front end of the running plate. His late Majesty rode on the footplate for some considerable mileages during the long journey across Canada, and he was so impressed with the performance of the engine that he consented to all the engines of the domeless-boilered series being known as 'Royal Hudsons'. They all subsequently had the coronet added. Technical details are given under reference 132.

130 Canadian Pacific Railway: 2-10-0 Bank Engine for Service in the Rocky Mountains.

Field, British Columbia, standing 4076 ft. above sea-level, is the central railway town of the mountain divisions of the C.P.R., and it is there that in steam days the bank, or 'helper', engines for the Field Hill were stationed. 'Hill' is a mild term for the tremendous gradient that has to be climbed by eastbound trains between Field and the Continental Divide at Stephen, 5337 ft. above sea-level. Even though the train engine is one of the enormous 2–10–4s (ref. 136), the trains sometimes have to be not double-headed but *triple* headed. The engine illustrated, used for 'pusher' or 'helper' work on the Hill, was one of a class originally built as 0–6 + 6–0 Mallet compounds. But however well Mallets may have done as bank engines elsewhere, notably on the Hex River Pass in South Africa, see reference 36, they were not a success on the Field Hill, and they were rebuilt into the strong, workmanlike engines in our picture, dispensing with all the articulation and the compounding and giving them just two cylinders 23½ in. diameter by 32 in. stroke, which with their 4 ft. 10 in. diameter driving wheels gave them a tractive effort of 51,800 lb. Like all locomotives working from Field, they were oil burners.

131 Canadian National Railways: 4–6–4 Express Locomotive.

In the year 1930 the increasing importance of the International route between Canada and the U.S.A., and the running of the crack trains operating between Montreal and Chicago, led to the introduction of some very fine new 4–6–4 locomotives designed for high-speed running. Students of British locomotive practice will note, however, the remarkable way in which the styling of these Canadian 4–6–4s anticipated the styling of the 'Britannia' class Pacifics of 1951. As usual in North America at that time, there were only two cylinders, 23 in. diameter by 28 in. stroke; the coupled wheels were 6 ft. 8 in. diameter; and the boiler, with a high steam pressure of 275 lb. per sq. in., was designed for continuous hard steaming. This evaporative heating surface was 3377 sq. ft.; the superheating surface 1492 sq. ft., and the grate area 73·6 sq. ft. The rated tractive force was 43,300 lb., to which the booster unit added 10,100 lb. when starting. These engines were designed for sustained hard running at high speed, on relatively level track, and in such service did very well. They were built in Canada by the Montreal Locomotive Works Ltd.

132 Canadian Pacific Railway: The '2800' 'Hudson' Class 4–6–4.

This class, introduced in 1928, was the progenitor of the famous 'Royal Hudsons' of 1937. Except for the section through the Rocky Mountains, engines of the 4–6–4 type worked the Transcontinental expresses through between the cities of the St Lawrence and the Pacific coast. From Montreal to Vancouver is 2882 miles by rail, and in steam days that journey time by the principal express trains was a little over 87 hours, an average of 33 m.p.h. including stops. These 'Hudsons' had two cylinders 22 in. diameter and 30 in. stroke, and the coupled wheels were of the relative large size of 6 ft. 3 in. The boiler pressure was 275 lb. per sq. in., and although they were colossal engines by British standards, weighing with their tenders 294 tons, their tractive effort was no more than 45,250 lb.—not so much greater than that of a GWR 'King' 4–6–0 of 135 tons. The CPR 'Hudsons' with their huge boilers were designed for continuous hard thrashing. They had mechanical stokers, as was very necessary with a grate area of 81 sq. ft. These engines handled trains of 1500 tons without assistance on the prairie sections of the line.

133 Norwegian State Railways: The 'Dovregubben' 2–8–4 Type Express Passenger Locomotive.

In 1936 some remarkable new four-cylinder compound 2–8–4 locomotives were introduced for working over the heavy gradients of the mountainous main line between Oslo and Trondjhem, which attains an altitude of about 3000 ft. north of Dombas. The choice of the 2–8–4 type for these powerful locomotives followed a definite trend in continental Europe at that time, and notable examples were to be seen in Austria, Rumania, and in the Soviet Union. The use of a four-wheeled trailing truck permits the use of a large wide firebox, without any hampering restrictions from the trailing coupled axle. It is also interesting that at a time when compounds were falling out of favour, except in France, that these engines were compounded. For heavy slogging on mountain grades such as those of the Dovre line, the compound has some advantages. These striking engines had high-pressure cylinders $18\frac{1}{4}$ in. diameter by $25\frac{5}{8}$ in. stroke; low-pressure cylinders $28\frac{3}{8}$ in. diameter by $27\frac{5}{8}$ in. stroke; the coupled-wheel diameter was 5 ft. 1 in., and the total weight of engine and tender in working order 150 tons.

134 Soviet Russian Railways: The 'IS' Class 2–8–4 Express Passenger Locomotive of 1932.

For routes that had been renewed with heavier rails, and where it was desired to accelerate passenger train services, a very large and powerful design of locomotive was worked out. A wheel arrangement of 4–8–2 was at first considered, but having regard to the very large firebox necessary,

mechanically stoked, the wheel arrangement was turned end for end, and eventually became 2–8–4. The outstanding success of the Austrian 2–8–4 (ref. 19) and its adoption as a standard in Rumania no doubt did not pass unnoticed in Russia. The new engines were known originally as the IS—'Iosif Stalin'—class, and the first examples were turned out from Kolomna Works in 1932–5. But when quantity production was authorized the work was done at the Voroshilovgrad works, and eventually the class numbered some 650 engines. One of these engines, magnificently turned out in a bright blue livery, was on display in Paris at an International exhibition in 1938. The great height of the Russian loading gauge permits of taller chimney and boiler mountings than elsewhere, and unless one is alongside, rather gives the impression that these locomotives are smaller than they actually are.

135 South Indian Railway: Indian Broad-gauge Standard 2–8–2 Freight Engine.

The standardization of locomotive types for the major Indian railways was a work of great importance, carried out as a joint project between the Indian Government, the British Engineering Standards Association (now the British Standards Institution), and the British locomotive building industry. The entire field of main-line passenger and freight working was surveyed with a view to establishing the minimum number of designs necessary to work the traffic on the State-owned railways. Reference is made elsewhere in this book to the 'XA', 'XB', and 'XC' passenger 'Pacific' engines, and how these did not meet all the requirements. Under reference 85, the variation in heavy express passenger locomotives under Class 'XS2' is illustrated. It was the same with freight locomotives. The 'XD' was the standard heavy goods 2–8–2; but larger varieties, in the form of the 'XD3' illustrated, were designed, in this particular instance for the South Indian Railway, and an even larger 2–8–2, designated 'XE', was used on some lines. They were all nevertheless very handsome locomotives, essentially British in their appearance.

136 **Canadian Pacific Railway:** The 2–10–4 Heavy Passenger Locomotive for Rocky Mountain Service.

Under reference 130, a type of helper engine used on the Field Hill was described. Our present subject is the train engine. These remarkable machines used to take over haulage of the transcontinental expresses at Calgary, and worked over the Field Hill section. They were oil burners, and with coupled wheels of only 5 ft. 3 in. diameter were specially suited to tremendously hard pounding on the mountain section. They had two cylinders 25 in. diameter by 32 in. stroke, and the boiler was appropriately very large, with 5054 sq. ft. of evaporative heating surface and 2032 sq. ft. of super-heating surface; the grate area was no less than $93\frac{1}{2}$ sq. ft. When working hard these locomotive gave an impression of colossal power, and ample evidence of heavy moving parts revolving rapidly. The total weight of engine and tender in working order was 330 tons, and a tractive effort of 89,000 lb. When express trains of 1500 tons had to be taken up the Field Hill, however, a single 2–10–2 'helper' was not always enough, and one had a 'Pacific' or a 2–10–0 leading a cavalcade of three locomotives.

137 **London and North Eastern Railway:** Triplet Articulated Dining-Car Set.

The fame of Sir Nigel Gresley as an engine designer is world-wide; but prior to his appointment as Locomotive Engineer of the Great Northern Railway in 1911 he was Carriage and Wagon Engineer, and during his tenure of office in that capacity he initiated a new principle in carriage construction by producing articulated stock. From the passengers' point of view these were two carriages closely coupled together; but instead of each carriage having its own bogies the assembly had only three bogies—one at each end, and one beneath the point of coupling of the two carriages. This not only produced a very smooth-riding pair of vehicles but it reduced the dead weight by that of one bogie. As Chief Mechanical Engineer of the L.N.E.R. he introduced triplet dining-car sets, with a separate kitchen car mounted between saloons for first- and third-class passengers respectively. There were only four bogies beneath three vehicles. These sets were used on the principal Anglo-Scottish expresses, and rode most luxuriously at high speed. From the weight haulage point of view the tare weight of a triplet set was 84 tons, whereas the total weight of three vehicles of conventional type would have been about 100 tons.

138 **International Sleeping Car Company:** Pullman Car for the 'Golden Arrow' Service in France.

The inauguration of the all-Pullman service between London and Paris, in 1927, was the result of a remarkable British enterprise. Sir Davidson Dalziel, Chairman of the Pullman Car Company in England, sensed the demand for a luxury day service between London and Paris long before the days of regular air travel, and he not only secured agreement from the French railway authorities to operate the joint service but by the international nature of the enterprise, paved the way for a British firm, the Leeds Forge Co. Ltd., to secure the contract to build the cars to be used on the French part of the journey! Structurally, and so far as bogies, couplings, brakes, and operating gear were concerned, the vehicles conformed to French standards, though the Leeds Forge Company had already gained experience in this direction in building sleeping cars for 'The Blue Train'. The interior décor, and the style of armchairs was, however, essentially English. It was certainly a delightful experience to travel from London to Paris by this service: from Victoria to Dover in standard English Pullmans, by 'The Golden Arrow', and then at Calais to entrain in the British-built French Pullmans of 'La Fleche d'Or'.

139 New Zealand Government Railways: Standard Second-class Main-line Coach.

Coaching stock was at one time a less advanced feature of these railways, but just at the end of our period some splendid new carriages of an entirely new design were added to the stock. They were a great advance upon the typical New Zealand coach of earlier days, with open-end platforms. They were of the steel, so-called 'wagon-top' design with large entrance vestibules. The seats, in both first- and second-class are of the reversible-back type, New Zealand having always followed American practice in this respect. Second-class seats followed the old traditions in shape, but the seats in the new first-class carriages, while retaining the walk-over back in a modified form,

rivalled in comfort the best European first-class seats. These cars created something of a sensation in a country so universally familiar with the open-platform coach. Its long use was no doubt due, in part, to the temperate climate of New Zealand, in which its disadvantages were much less than where extremes of climate are experienced. With the introduction of the new cars there began a gradual change towards uniformity in appearance of passenger rolling stock, as a comparison between French, German, Belgian, and New Zealand coaches shows.

140 Denver and Rio Grande Western: Narrow Gauge 2–8–2 Locomotive of Class K-36.

This railroad cuts through some of the most mountainous country in the whole of the United States. Its main line extends from Denver in Colorado to Salt Lake City, a distance of 745 miles. Originally it was entirely narrow gauge, but since conversion, and through its connections at the eastern and western extremities, it now forms part of one of the great transcontinental routes. In the 1920s out of a total of 2562 route miles, some 800 were still narrow gauge, 3 ft. 0 in. The exceedingly heavy gradients, sharp curvature on the lines that thread a way through deep canyons, and wild mountain passes in the heart of the Rockies demand high-capacity motive power, and in 1925 the Baldwin Locomotive Works built a batch of 2–8–2 locomotives having the high tractive effort, for the narrow gauge, of 36,200 lb. Our picture shows one of these smart little engines, which even so, weigh nearly 145 tons with their tenders. They were put to work on the freight trains between Salida, where the narrow gauge joins the main line, and Gunnison, between which is the notorious Marshall Pass with its long gradient of 1 in 25. Unassisted, the Class K-36 2-8-2s could handle trains of 230 tons; but to handle the traffic offered at that time single-train loads of 600 tons were necessary, and up the 1 in 25 of the Marshall Pass it was usual to have *three* engines, two at the front, and one banking in rear.

141 **Nigerian Railways:** 4-8-0 Type Mixed Traffic Locomotive.

Among the railways of West Africa, working their way inland from ports on the Atlantic Ocean, the Nigerian provides a typical example, on the 3 ft. 6 in. gauge, laid with relatively light rails; and this severely limited the weight that can be accepted on any axle. At the same time, in studying the equipment and methods of operation, one must lay aside all European and American concepts of high speed and frequency of traffic. Such railways were built in the first place through a terrain where nothing previously existed, save jungle tracks, and the main thing was to secure some means of reliable mechanical transportation. The smart little 4-8-0 locomotive illustrated and built by Robert Stephenson and Hawthorn's Ltd. was of a type ideal for the job. It followed the Cape and Rhodesian tradition of using the 4-8-0 type wheel arrangement in preference to the 'Pacific'; for although the presence of coupled wheels at the rear end limited the size of firebox, the eight-coupled wheels provided an excellent machine for getting away with a reasonably heavy load. The principal dimensions were: cylinders 18 in. diameter by 23 in. stroke; coupled wheels 4 ft. diameter; boiler pressure 160 lb. per sq. in; total weight of engine and tender in working order 84·9 tons; tractive effort 21,114 lb.

142 **South African Railways:** The Class '16C' 'Pacific' Express Locomotive of 1919.

This class of 'Pacific', introduced for the long-distance passenger workings over the more level stretches of line, represents the culmination of a long chain of development of the Pacific type in South Africa, beginning on the former Central South African Railway in 1904. There was a gradual increase in weight and tractive power from Class '10' of 1904, weighing 70·6 tons without tender and having a tractive effort of 23,180 lb., to the '16C', weighing 82½ tons and having a tractive effort of 29,890 lb. The '16C' was the last 'Pacific' design to have the 'small' type of boiler, with a heating surface of 2000 sq. ft. and a grate area of 36 sq. ft. From the '16C' to the '16D' was a tremendous jump in boiler capacity, and from that time the 'big-engine' era in South Africa can be considered to have started. Nevertheless, the '16C' and its predecessors of the '16A' and '16B' classes still had a great amount of useful work to do, and many are still in service today. The standard livery of the S.A.R. is black, but great pride is taken in the locomotives, and one finds little touches of gay colour added to certain parts by the individual crews. In our picture the engine is shown with the axle-ends and hand-rail knobs painted red.

143 **Mysore State Railway:** Metre Gauge 'Pacific' Locomotive.

The Indian railways are laid on three separate gauges—5 ft. 6 in., metre, and 2 ft. This was not a case, as in Australia, of lines being built by independent decision, without regard to what was happening elsewhere in the country, but on a definite overall plan, dictated to some extent in the early stages by strategic considerations, stipulated by the military authorities. The metre and 2-ft.-gauge lines were built as feeders to the broad-gauge lines, where the cost of construction did not justify full broad-gauge standards, due to difficulty of terrain or infrequency of service. Some very fine locomotives have, nevertheless, been designed for the sub-standard-gauge lines, and an excellent example is provided by the Mysore 'Pacific', the subject of our picture. Without referring to the actual dimensions, the massive well-proportioned appearance gives the impression of a heavy main-line 'Pacific', but in actual fact it is quite a 'baby', with the engine alone weighing no more than 50 tons, and having a tractive effort roughly half that of an 'XC' 5 ft. 6 in. gauge express passenger 'Pacific'. The cylinders were 16 in. diameter by 23 in. stroke; coupled-wheel diameter 4 ft. 9 in.; boiler pressure 180 lb. per sq. in.; and tractive effort, 16,492 lb. These engines were built by Robert Stephenson and Hawthorn's Ltd.

144 Baltimore and Ohio Railroad: An Anglicised 'Pacific' Locomotive of 1928.

In the year 1927 this famous American railroad celebrated its centenary with a great pageant of railway history, and to this exhibition the Great Western Railway of England was invited to send a locomotive. As related under reference 1 of this book, the English representative was none other than the *King George V*, then brand new. Its neat outline and beautiful finish created an immense impression in the U.S.A., particularly as the trial runs subsequently made showed that this most elegant engine was capable of very hard and fast running. Reaction to the design

itself on the Baltimore and Ohio Railroad was most interesting. Within the year a new type of 'Pacific' locomotive had been built, in which a notable degree of 'tidying up' had been incorporated. Pipes and fittings were discreetly hidden, and an attempt was made to copy the Great Western style of chimney, with its famous copper cap. Though still distinctly American in its general appearance, with high raised running plate exposing all of the wheels, and the large sand-box on the forward ring of the boiler, it was certainly a handsome and successful design.

145 Baltimore and Ohio Railroad: Lightweight High-speed 4-4-4 Locomotive of 1934.

For some time following the Centenary celebrations of 1927, when the English locomotive *King George V* visited the U.S.A. (ref. 1), the practice of this railroad had some affinity to that of the Great Western Railway of England. The 'Anglicized' Pacific has already been described (ref. 144), and it is probable that the experimental locomotive shown in the present illustration was to some extent inspired by the spectacular running of the 'Cheltenham Flyer' (ref. 43). In this American 4-4-4 the coupled wheels were made 7 ft. diameter for high-speed running, and by use of the Emerson type of water-tube firebox the exceptionally high steam pressure of 350 lb. per sq. in. was used, in conjunction with a mechanical stoker. By American standards the physical size of the boiler was not large, having an evaporative heating surface of 1780 sq. ft., superheating surface of 415 sq. ft., and a grate area of 61·8 sq. ft.; but the very high boiler pressure boosted the tractive effort to 28,000 lb. Evidence of Great Western influence is seen in the copper-capped chimney. At that time, however, there was insufficient lightweight traffic to justify building more locomotives of this type, and although successful, this 4-4-4 remained an isolated, though fascinating, example.

146 Chicago, Milwaukee, St Paul, and Pacific Railroad: Streamlined 4-4-2 Locomotive for the 'Hiawatha' Express.

These striking locomotives, among the first to be fully streamlined, and designed specially for high-speed express work, were built in 1935 by the American Locomotive Company. The 'Hiawatha' express was scheduled to cover the 421 miles of water-level route between Chicago and Minneapolis in the even 7 hours, with five intermediate stops. Continuous running at 100 m.p.h. was needed over lengthy stretches of level track, and the original load of the train was six heavy cars weighing about 350 tons behind the tender. Every modern development of the period was built into these locomotives. The coupled wheels were 7 ft. diameter, the boiler pressure 300 lb. per sq. in., and the boiler itself with 3245 sq. ft. of evaporative heating surface, 1029 sq. ft. of superheating surface, and 69 sq. ft. of grate area was enormous for an engine of the 'Atlantic' type. It was reported that during preliminary trials speeds up to 128 m.p.h. were noted on the speedometer, but no complete verification of such speeds has been made subsequently. There is no doubt, however, that they were extremely fast-running locomotives. Their life was nevertheless very short. The train proved so popular that many extra coaches were added to the load, and special new locomotives of the 4-6-4 type designed to run it.

147 New York Central Lines: Streamlined 4-6-4 Locomotive for the 'Twentieth Century Limited'.

The New York Central pioneered the use of the 4-6-4 type in the U.S.A. for heavy express passenger working, the first examples being built by the American Locomotive Company in 1927. This road is fortunate in having an almost level main line throughout from New York to Chicago, following first the Hudson River, and then the shores of the great lakes. From the original 4-6-4 of 1927, which proved to have vastly greater haulage capacity than the existing 'Pacifics', the type was developed to the very fine version illustrated, and built, also by A.L.C.O., in 1938. Working of the 'Twentieth Century Limited' involved the hauling of loads in excess of 1000 tons at speeds of 80 m.p.h. on level track, and these strikingly styled streamlined locomotives had two cylinders $22\frac{1}{2}$ in. diameter by 29 in. stroke, coupled wheels 6 ft. 7 in. diameter, and a boiler with an evaporative heating surface of 4187 sq. ft., superheating surface of 1745 sq. ft., and a grate area of 81·5 sq. ft. The boiler pressure was 275 lb. per sq. in. The tractive effort was only moderate, 43,400 lb., but these engines were an outstanding success in the duty for which they were designed; the punctuality of 'The Century'—as it was known—was proverbial. These great engines, with their tenders, weighed 260 tons. The tenders, loaded, were actually heavier than the engines.

148 Great Western Railway: 'Castle' Class 4-6-0 Partially Streamlined.

In the references to railways in many parts of the world the prevalent vogue of streamlining in the 1930s causes frequent comment. The locomotive department of the Great Western Railway was not interested in any such fashions, but certain directors felt that a Company with such a reputation for being in the forefront ought to show it was 'with it' in this trend, and the Chief Mechanical Engineer was instructed to streamline some locomotives for experimental purposes. The science of aeronautics had shown that it was not so much the direct forward resistance as the eddies behind projections that cause air resistance to motion, and his treatment of the 'Castle' engine, while not very edifying, underlined the principles involved. It was not considered worth while designing a full aerodynamic screening for the entire engine and tender. Whatever reduction in air resistance may have effected, a big disadvantage soon showed, in that the shrouding over the cylinders gave rise to heating in the motion work of the inside valve gear, and this shrouding was soon taken off. Similar treatment was also applied to one of the 'King' class 4–6–0s. The results were quite negative, and all the fairings except the wedge-fronted cabs were eventually taken off both engines.

149 **London and North Eastern Railway:** Streamlined 'Sandringham' Class 4–6–0.

On the L.N.E.R. full streamlining was applied with spectacular results to the Silver Jubilee train in 1935. By how much the performance and speedworthiness of that train could be traced directly to the streamlining has never been precisely ascertained, because there were never identical locomotives without the streamlined outer casing. Publicity wise, however, the effect was electrifying! The form of the

'Pacific' engines can be seen by referring to a later one of the same type, described and illustrated under reference 179 in this book. When it was decided, in 1939, to introduce a new luxury train between London and Norwich, to be called 'The East Anglian', Sir Nigel Gresley took two of the standard 'Sandringham' class three-cylinder 4–6–0s and streamlined them in the style of the 'A4' high-speed 'Pacifics'. From the performance point of view there was no need for this, because the train did not run to a very fast schedule, and the load was not heavy; but as a gesture it was much appreciated. The coaching stock of the train was finished in the standard L.N.E.R. varnished teak, and so the locomotive was painted in the standard apple-green livery. Only two engines were so treated. They were named specially *East Anglian* and *City of London*.

150 **London, Midland and Scottish Railway:** 'Coronation' Streamlined 'Pacific' with Casing Opened to Give Access to Smokebox.

The streamlining of steam locomotives gave rise to many problems in working. It is one thing to put a scientifically designed casing round the outside to minimize the air resistance when running at high speed; but one had also to consider the possible effects upon the machinery of cutting off the natural flow of air due to the speed, and the considerable reduction in the natural ventilation and cooling that can result. Another very important factor was that the shrouding interfered with access to the working parts for inspection and routine lubrication. Special inspection doors had to be provided in the streamlined casing; of these none looked stranger, when opened, than those giving access to the smokebox, as shown in our picture. In general, it was necessary to open the smokebox doors after every run, to shovel out the accumulation of ash and char that collects in the course of a long run. By 1940 various forms of self-cleaning smoke-boxes were being introduced by the use of which the doors did not need to be opened more than once a week, and even longer. But in the exigencies of wartime working all the L.M.S.R. streamlined casings were completely removed.

151 London and North Eastern Railway: The 'P1' Class 2–8–2 Heavy Mineral Engine.

The success of the original Great Northern Railway 'Pacifics' introduced in 1922 led Sir Nigel Gresley to apply the large and free-steaming boiler to a heavy mineral engine, in 1925. At that time the coal traffic between Peterborough and London was enormous, and it was thought that by the use of locomotives of greatly enhanced power some relief to the congestion of traffic might be provided by running considerably longer trains and fewer of them. Two of these strikingly handsome freight engines were built for experimental purposes. Loads of 1600 tons were worked with reliability, but trains of 100 wagons were something of a liability to the traffic department, because certain of the goods loops and yard tracks were not long enough, and special arrangements had to be made for the working of such long trains. These engines had a tractive effort of 38,500 lb., and took loads of 1600 tons, against 1300 tons by the standard 2–8–0 engines. But the operating diffi-culties, added to the falling off in traffic due to trade recession after 1928, led to the experiment being abandoned, and no further 2–8–2 mineral engines were built.

152 Northern Railway of France: 2–10–0 Compound Freight Engine.

The tenure of office of Monsieur Georges Collin as Chief Mechanical Engineer of this railway saw some striking develop-ments in locomotive practice. The super-Pacific has already been illustrated and described in this book (ref. 2), but the developments were no less interesting in regard to heavy freight locomotives. Two classes were standardized, having wheel arrangements of the 2–8–0 and 2–10–0 type, and both were four-cylinder com-pounds, generally on the de Glehn system. The 2–10–0, illustrated in our picture, was a very powerful engine designed for haul-ing trains of 1700 tons on a rising gradient of 1 in 200. The high-pressure cylinders, outside, drove on to the central pair of coupled wheels, while the inside low-pressure cylinders drove on to the second pair. The boiler was slightly smaller than that of the express passenger 'Pacific' engines, but of generally the same design. With coupled wheels of 5 ft. 1 in. diameter, these engines were capable of fast freight duties as well as hard-slogging slow service with maximum-tonnage coal trains. Their tractive effort when working full com-pound was 56,440 lb., and the total weight of engine alone in working order was $99\frac{3}{4}$ tons. They were very successful and long-lived engines.

153 Great Northern Railway of U.S.A.: Class 'R2' 2–8–8–2 of 1929.

For the most part American locomotives in the period under review were painted in unrelieved black. The only touches of colour on certain railroads were the company's emblems, and against the vast size of most express passenger and freight locomotives those emblems were little more than a speck! It is interesting to recall therefore the very pleasing livery of light green used on the Great Northern, and it certainly gave such enormous locomotives as the 'R2' class an air of most unusual distinction. They were designed primarily for heavy freight service in the Rocky Mountains, and were rated to haul loads of 4000 tons at 10 m.p.h. on a gradient of 1 in 100. They were extremely heavy and powerful engines with four cylinders, 26 in. diameter by 32 in. stroke; coupled-wheel diameter of 5 ft. 3 in., and a total weight in working order of 307 tons. The tender fully loaded with coal and water weighed another 166 tons. The boiler was exceptionally large, with 7834 sq. ft. of evaporative heating surface and 3515 sq. ft. superheater. On the basis of tractive effort these engines were the most powerful to run anywhere in the world, and the rated effort was 146,710 lb.—65 tons! On level track they were limited to a maximum speed of 40 m.p.h.

154 **German State Railways:** Class '50' 2–10–0 Heavy Freight Locomotive.

This remarkable design dates from 1938, in which year the first examples were built by Henschel. It was prepared as a general-service class, with a maximum axle load of only $15\frac{1}{2}$ tons, and so able to run over practically every line in the German railway system. They were nevertheless powerful locomotives with a rated tractive effort of 50,770 lb. The cylinders were 23·6 in. diameter by 26 in. stroke, and the coupled-wheel diameter 4 ft. 7 in. They were designed as general-purpose locomotives, with a maximum allowed speed of 50 m.p.h. They proved very successful and formed the basis of the German and Austrian wartime austerity classes. These differed from the original engines of 1938

only in detail. In all, no fewer than 10,650 of them were built, many by Austrian firms, and they handled a very high proportion of the total wartime traffic. A large number of them are still in service today, and the majority of the Austrian examples are now fitted with the Giesl oblong ejector. Since the war a number of locomotives of the same general design have been built for service in East Germany. They constitute the largest steam-locomotive group ever to have existed in the world.

155 **Egyptian State Railways:** 4–6–0 Express Passenger Locomotive.

The Egyptian State Railways were extensive users of the 'Atlantic' type of locomotive. The principal main lines, and particularly that between Cairo and Alexandria, are almost devoid of gradients, and at the moderate speeds scheduled 'Atlantics' gave a very economical performance. The start-to-stop speeds scheduled did not exceed 50 m.p.h. These moderate speeds were in recognition of the running difficulty in working against the prevailing wind in the Nile delta, where the line is completely exposed. In the 1930s, however, there was a desire to accelerate the principal expresses to start-to-stop average speed of 55 m.p.h. This had to be done while not exceeding the overall speed limit of 62 m.p.h. On routes of such uniform grading, or rather the absence of it, no difficulty was experienced in keeping the faster end-to-end times provided one could run steadily at 60–62 m.p.h. throughout, and to give enhanced reliability with greater adhesion, a number of the existing 'Atlantics' were converted into 4–6–0s, and had their boiler pressure raised from 160 to 180 lb. per sq. in. These conversions were a great success, and with the modified engines finished in the handsome style shown in our picture there was dignity as well as efficiency in the working of the accelerated trains.

156 Kenya and Uganda Railway: 2–8–2 Mail Train Engine.

The extreme physical difficulties of this mountain railway, in its long and severe gradients coupled with continuous curvature has made the operation of passenger and freight traffic a great problem, as traffic developed, and it was necessary to operate heavy trains. Before the railway became finally converted to use of the Beyer–Garratt type of articulated locomotives for the heaviest duties a very fine 'ordinary' type of locomotive was introduced for the mail trains, both east and west of Nairobi. The 2–8–2 type illustrated was built by Robert Stephenson and Hawthorns Ltd., and was an extremely powerful unit for the metre gauge, with a maximum axle-load of 17 tons. The two cylinders were $21\frac{1}{4}$ in. diameter by 28 in. stroke; coupled-wheel diameter 4 ft. 3 in., and boiler pressure 180 lb. per sq. in. The total weight of engine and tender in working order was 156 tons, and the tractive effort 37,938 lb. When originally introduced these engines were finished in the black livery then standard; but they are illustrated here as in their final days, in a livery precisely that of the former London Midland and Scottish Railway. After a long and arduous life they have recently been scrapped.

157 Indian Government Railway: The 'XA' Class Standard Broad-gauge Light 'Pacific'.

The range of Indian standard designs of 'Pacific' engine is illustrated under reference 83, for the 'XB' intermediate class, while the 'XS2' (ref. 85) illustrates a development of the standard 'XC' heavy Pacific. The 'XA' engine, which is the subject of our present picture was specially designed for branch-line passenger work on routes where the maximum axle-load was limited to 13 tons. It is a straightforward two-cylinder single-expansion engine, with a large boiler and firebox to cope with low-grade Indian coal. Large numbers of these locomotives were built by the Vulcan Foundry for the major Indian railways, which were under Government control in the 1930s. The majority were allocated to the North-Western Railway, and to the Great Indian Peninsular Railway. The cylinders are 18 in. diameter by 26 in. stroke; coupled-wheel diameter 5 ft. $1\frac{1}{2}$ in.; the total weight of engine and tender in working order is only $110\frac{3}{4}$ tons, while the tractive effort is 20,960 lb. They are very simple and straightforward engines, both for operating and maintenance, and have proved very successful in service. Unlike the larger standard 'Pacifics' of the 'XB', 'XC', and 'XS' classes, the 'XA', by reason of their reduced range of workings, have six-wheeled tenders, and not the large-bogie type.

158 Gold Coast Railways: 4–6–2 Passenger and Mail Locomotive.

The railways of the Gold Coast (now Ghana) are laid to the 3 ft. 6 in. used in South Africa, and include no more than a relatively light permanent way. The maximum axle-load of the handsome 'Pacific' locomotive we illustrate is only 12·5 tons, and despite its impressive proportions, it is no more than a relatively small and light power unit. It is one of a series built by Beyer Peacock and Company. The two cylinders were no more than 18 in. diameter by 26 in. stroke, and the coupled wheels 5 ft. 0 in. diameter. The total weight of engine and tender in working order is only 107¾ tons, and the tractive effort 21,000 lb. The design, although generally British in character, includes bar frames and other features calculated to keep the weight to a minimum. The firebox, having a grate area of 25 sq. ft., is relatively large in relation to the general proportions of the locomotive, and is arranged for burning local coal, which is not of a high quality compared with that contemporarily available in Great Britain. The engines of this class have rendered excellent service, and constitute a fine example of British designing to meet special overseas conditions.

159 **Norfolk and Western Railway:** The Class 'J' 4–8–4 Express Passenger Locomotive.

This line, which was one of the few in America to use the name 'railway' instead of 'railroad', was one of the last to place complete reliance upon steam power for its train services, and the 'J' was developed in direct opposition to the general advance of diesel traction. It was designed for the hardest and fastest duty imaginable, to work maximum-tonnage trains over mountain grades, and to run at 100 m.p.h. elsewhere. Special attention was given to ease of servicing, and the locomotives were regularly scheduled to run 4000 miles per week. All axles had roller bearings, also on the big-ends and crankpins. The general proportions were very large, with two cylinders 27 in. diameter by 32 in. stroke, coupled wheels 5 ft. 10 in. diameter, a boiler pressure of 275 lb. per sq. in., and a tractive effort of 73,300 lb. The total weight of engine and tender in work-

ing order was 395 tons. The fuel was coal. The great success of these engines was due particularly to the thoroughly modern arrangements for servicing which the Norfolk and Western Railway installed, and to the determination of its management to make the best use of the coal that was readily available within the railway's own territory.

160 **Buenos Aires Great Southern Railway:** The '12K' Two-cylinder 'Pacific' of 1939.

At the very end of the period covered by this book the Vulcan Foundry delivered locomotives of the 4–6–2 and 4–8–0 types to the B.A.G.S. Railway. The two classes looked very similar, having the same design of boiler and firebox, and similar cylinders and motion: two cylinders only, 19 in. diameter by 28 in. stroke. The 4–8–0 had previously been supplied to the Buenos Aires Western Railway, and thus it could be said that the latter was really the progenitor of these two new B.A.G.S. classes. The '12K' Pacific, having 6-ft.-diameter coupled wheels, was intended for heavy intermediate traffic rather than the fastest expresses. The boilers steamed well, and in the class of service just mentioned the new engines did well. On the faster trains they proved sluggish, but a re-design of the cylinder exhaust passages made a great difference, and speeds of 70 m.p.h. on level track, with trailing loads of 400 tons became commonplace. Our picture shows one of these engines in its original condition, with smoke-deflecting plates on either side of the smokebox. These were eventually found to be unnecessary and were taken off. Other leading dimensions were, coupled wheels 6 ft. diameter; grate area 32·6 sq. ft.; boiler pressure 225 lb. per sq. in.; total weight of engine and tender in working order 156·9 tons; tractive effort 25,270 lb.

161 South African Railways: The '15F' Class 4–8–2 Mixed Traffic Locomotive.

On the railways of the world there are a few outstanding types of locomotive that are universal favourites. On British Railways we had the Stanier 'Black-five' 4–6–0 (ref. 95); its counterpart in South Africa, though a much larger engine, is the '15F'. A total of 255 of these magnificent machines are in service, and they tackle anything from heavy express passenger trains, over the long and undulating stretches of the Veldt, to hard, slogging freight duties in the Transvaal, and in the Eastern Cape Province. Some of the heaviest freight trains are made up to such enormous lengths that '15F' engines are used in pairs! Technically they are a development of the '15CA', with a larger boiler, and cylinders 24 in. diameter and 28 in. stroke. The coupled wheels are 5 ft. diameter, and the weight of engine and tender together in working order is 177¾ tons. Great pride is taken in the smart appearance of these engines. The copper pipework is always kept highly burnished; some individual engines have their smokeboxes distinguished by aluminium paint, and the drivers add little touches of decoration to the smokebox doors, such as leaping animals, cut out of sheet copper.

162 Rhodesia Railways: The 15th Class 4–6–4 + 4–6–4 Fast Passenger and Mail 'Garratt'.

The Rhodesia Railways in its diversity of main lines has rather different operating conditions than those of the railways in certain neighbouring countries. On the three principal routes—Bulawayo to Salisbury and Umtali, Bulawayo to the Victoria Falls, and Bulawayo southwards into South Africa—there is not the same incidence of long and severe gradients, and a locomotive capable of faster running was desirable. Just before the war an order was placed for four locomotives of the 4–6–4 + 4–6–4 type, intended originally for the south run through Bechuanaland, or Botswana as it is now known, from Bulawayo to Mafeking; but actually under the extreme pressure of wartime traffic these four engines were used between Bulawayo and Salisbury. These engines gave remarkable results, both in actual haulage power and reliability. They quickly became known as the greyhounds of the Rhodesia Railways stud, though of course this does not mean they attained speeds of 60, 70, or 80 m.p.h.! But they were very free-running, and immensely popular with their crews. These engines had cylinders 17½ in. diameter by 26 in. stroke; coupled wheels 4 ft. 9 in. diameter, a grate area of 49½ sq. ft., and the total weight in working order is 179½ tons. The tractive effort at 85 per cent boiler pressure is 42,750 lb. The four original engines, of which our picture shows the pioneer, No. 272, were so successful that a further 70 were added to the stock after the war, and they now constitute the largest individual locomotive class on the line.

163 Northern Railway of France: 2–8–2 Suburban Passenger Tank Engine.

In the early 1930s special attention was being given by several of the French railways to the improvement of the outer suburban service around Paris. The building of new dormitory suburbs, with large blocks of flats, was resulting in large numbers of commuters entering and leaving Paris morning and evening. Traffic developed along the existing main railway lines, and powerful new locomotives were required. The Northern company created something of a sensation by reverting to single-expansion locomotives for this arduous duty—all modern types being otherwise exclusively compounds. The new 2-8-2s had many features and accessories similar to the main-line express 'Pacifics' (ref. 2), but had two cylinders only $25\frac{3}{16}$ in. diameter by $27\frac{9}{16}$ in. stroke. They were designed for rapid acceleration from rest, with heavy trains, and proved a great success, hauling loads up to 475 tons at 70 m.p.h. on a rising 1 in 200 gradient. To avoid light running at the terminal points the engines were not uncoupled from their trains. The driver transferred to the opposite end of the train, and regulated the working of the engine by remote control. Only the fireman remained on the footplate for this reverse direction of running.

164 Buenos Aires Pacific Railway: 4-6-4 Suburban Passenger Tank Engine.

The suburban traffic around Buenos Aires grew to immense proportions in the 1920s, and the B.A.P.R. like the B.A.G.S. Railway had to introduce larger and more powerful locomotives to cope with longer and heavier trains. Like the B.A.G.S., the 'Pacific' used three-cylinder simple engines, of great power, and our picture shows the very handsome, typically British design, constructed by Robert Stephenson and Hawthorns Ltd., in 1930. These engines had three cylinders 19 in. diameter by 26 in. stroke; coupled wheels 5 ft. 7 in. diameter, and worked at a pressure of 200 lb. per sq. in. At that time a considerable tonnage of Welsh coal was imported

into the Argentine for locomotive use, and these engines, with a grate area of only 27 sq. ft., were designed for working on good-quality soft British coal. Although the boilers and fireboxes were relatively small, they were otherwise large and heavy engines with a total weight in working order of $128\frac{1}{4}$ tons, and a high tractive effort of 35,722 lb. The track permitted a high axle loading, and with an adhesion weight of 64 tons the engines were ideally suited to rapid acceleration from stops with heavy trains.

165 Southern Railway (England): 2-6-4 Fast Passenger Tank Engine.

Among a group of tank engines designed for fast suburban passenger and other short-distance working, this Southern 2-6-4 requires special notice. It was introduced by the former South Eastern and Chatham Railway, and was originally intended for the residential express trains between London and the Kent Coast towns, none of which had non-stop runs of more than about 70 miles. It was the first British passenger tank engine of the 2-6-4 type. The engine illustrated was actually the S.E. & C.R. prototype, and a number of engines of the class were built after grouping and used with success, not only on the S.E. & C.R. line but also on the former Brighton line. Unfortunately one of them was involved in a serious derailment near Sevenoaks in 1927, and although the condition of the track was subsequently considered the major cause of the accident, the locomotives of this class were converted to 2-6-0 tender engines. Nevertheless, although the 2-6-4 did not survive as a tank engine on the Southern, it was adopted and developed with great success on the London Midland and Scottish Railway, and the latter development was eventually extended into the standard steam locomotive range of the nationalized British Railways.

166 Buenos Aires Great Southern Railway: The Class '8E' Three-cylinder 2-6-4 Tank Engine.

This class was introduced from 1923 onwards to cope with the enormous suburban traffic around Buenos Aires. They were the first three-cylinder simple engines to be purchased, and the first to have crank axles on the B.A.G.S. Railway. Eventually there were 61 of the class: the first 12 by Hawthorn, Leslie and Co.; 15 by North British Locomotive Co. Ltd.; another 15 by Vulcan, in 1926-7; and the remainder also by Vulcan in 1930. The cylinders were $17\frac{1}{2}$ in. diameter by 26 in. stroke, each with its own set of Walschaerts valve gear; coupled wheels were 5 ft. 8 in. diameter, and the working pressure 200 lb. per sq. in. The weight of these large tank engines in working order was 101 tons. After a very hard life, giving excellent service, the management, in 1949, thought that painting the locomotives in colours, instead of the standard black, would lead to better care being taken of them. Four of the '8E' engines were painted in colours similar to certain pre-grouping British railways: one in Caledonian blue, one in Midland red, one in North British olive, and one in North Eastern green. The North British 'olive' was chosen, but it did not have the desired effect, and there was soon a reversion to black, with yellow lines, as previously.

167 Buenos Aires Great Southern Railway: Gantry of Upper-quadrant Signals.

The Argentine railways during the period under review in this book were pre-dominantly British in their equipment, and on this account it might appear strange that in the modernization of the great terminal station of Plaza Constitution the B.A.G.S. Railway should have adopted so typically American a design as that illustrated in our picture, in 1925. At that time, however, the upper-quadrant signal, working in three positions, was being introduced to a limited extent in England, and it was not until the publication of the report of the Three-Position Signal Committee of the Institution of Railway Signal Engineers in 1925 that the colour-light type of signal was adopted as the future British standard, rather than the three-position upper-quadrant semaphore. The installation at Plaza Constitution, in Buenos Aires, was therefore something of a period piece, and it was in fact the largest of its kind ever installed by a British contractor. The signals are interesting, in that the mechanisms were electro-pneumatic. The aspects displayed and their meaning are:

Horizontal	'stop'
Inclined upwards at 45 deg.	'caution'
Pointing vertically upwards	'clear'

168 Southern Railway (England): Colour-light Signals and Route Indicators at Waterloo.

This illustration typifies British development in power signalling up to the year 1937. The group is one of the platform starting signals at Waterloo, relating to platform roads to left and right of the signal post. Each group has a main running signal of the colour-light type, showing as required, red for 'stop', yellow for 'caution', and green for 'all clear'. In contrast to the Argentine gantry under reference 167, there is only one signal for each road, and the route to be taken at the junctions ahead is not indicated by a geographical disposition of separate arms but by a route indicator. This is of the so-called 'theatre-sign' type, in which the indication is produced by selecting appropriate lamps on the display ground. At the time this installation was put in service many trains at Waterloo were hauled by steam locomotives, and after the departure of the train the engine which had brought in the empty coaches and stood during loading time at the buffers drew out after the train had departed, and waited at the outer end of the platform for further instructions. The banner signal beside the main unit was used to authorize a shunt movement. These were plain discs, rotated electrically, and floodlit at night from the small light unit poised just above the disc itself.

169 **London, Midland and Scottish Railway:** Electric Banner Signals at St Enoch Station, Glasgow.

From a very early date in railway signalling engineers and operating men have been concerned to provide a clear distinction between signals authorizing a main-line movement, and those permitting no more than a shunt, or a limited move. In many places in mechanical days no signals at all were provided to indicate shunt movements. There were usually a number of men employed in the station yards, and it was quite usual for shunting to be controlled either by hand signals or by word of mouth. With the introduction of power working, and the signalmen often regulating movements over parts of the line they could actually see, the older methods were no longer applicable. The picture reference 168 shows a form of shunt signal used on the Southern Railway; our present picture shows an earlier type, namely the Sykes electrically worked

banner signal contained in a glass-fronted case and internally illuminated at night. The actual bar was red. These signals shown in our picture were at one time installed at St Enoch station, Glasgow, at the entrance to the platforms, and authorized a driver to proceed cautiously into the station and up to the buffer stops.

170 **Victorian Railways:** Gantry of Somersault Arms, Flinders Street Station, Melbourne.

In an earlier book in this general series of colour books, *British Steam Railways*, reference was made to the distinctive Great Northern Railway type of semaphore: the centre-balanced, or somersault, type evolved after the serious accident at Abbots Ripton in 1876. The British signalling firm of McKenzie and Holland, of Worcester, adopted the somersault arm as one of their standard products, and it was used on a number of the Welsh railways, and in Northern Ireland. McKenzie and Holland Ltd. formed a subsidiary company in Australia, and it was through them that the somersault arm was introduced and became standard on the Victorian Railways. Our pictures show a tremendous array of them on a gantry outside the great terminus of Flinders Street, Melbourne, one of the busiest city stations anywhere in the world. Where mechanical working is retained the somersault arm remains standard in Victoria today. The disc signals shown on the same gantry provide another example of the distinction necessary between main and shunt movements. They have a small red light in the centre when indicating 'stop'. They are rotated sideways through an angle of 90 deg. to clear. Then the red target appears 'on edge' only, and a small green light is exhibited.

171 Belgian National Railways: First- and Second-class Composite Carriage for International Service.

Belgium has a very intense network of railways, and while many of the routes are concerned with high-density commuter traffic and inter-city fast trains within the country itself, a large proportion of the main-line train services are international, and include connections to many distant parts of Europe. Some of the most celebrated of the international trains are those running non-stop between Brussels and Paris, without any halt at the Franco-Belgian frontier. In the mid-1930s the Belgian railways designed and built an entirely new series of all-steel rolling stock, covering requirements not only for international but also for internal passenger traffic. Our picture shows one of the fine composite carriages for international service. Generally speaking, the coaching stock in use on the continent of Europe has not been distinguished by any very attractive styles of painting, such as was characteristic of the British railways in pre-nationalization days; but the new Belgian coaches were certainly a very pleasant exception, and made their country of origin instantly recognizable in trains containing through carriages of many nations.

172 Canadian National Railways: Air-conditioned Coach.

Just before the outbreak of the Second World War the Canadian National Railways took delivery of some fine new passenger stock that was air-conditioned on the ice-actuated system. At that time air-conditioning was generally considered a luxury, though in retrospect one can only guess at the conditions of travel in hot, dry countries in days before its general intro-

duction on important long-distance trains. These Canadian National cars were first class, and of the open-saloon type seating 64 passengers, arranged in pairs on either side of a central gangway. They were very comfortably appointed with Dunlopillo upholstery, though the general interior effect was more that of a modern airliner than the British conception of a first-class railway coach. They were large and heavy vehicles, although the numbers of first-class passengers seated were also large. The length over buffers was 83 ft. $3\frac{1}{2}$ in., the overall width 9 ft. 11 in., and the tare weight 60 tons. The accommodation included separate lavatories for men and women, and also a women's retiring room.

173 Danish State Railways: All-steel Refrigerator Van.

The Danish State Railway system is a difficult one to operate on account of its extending over the several islands contained in the Danish archipelago, and on the mainland of Jutland, with connection by train ferries. The equipment is modern, and services of both passenger and freight trains include international through workings. The State Railway owns some 14,000 freight vehicles, most of which are of the typical Continental long-wheelbased four-wheeled type, which can be safely run at speeds of 50 m.p.h. and more. All are fitted with the continuous automatic air brake of the Knorr type—a Continental derivation of the Westinghouse. The vehicle in our picture is of a modern design of all-steel refrigerator van, which like those used for all forms of perishable goods is painted white. The colour for ordinary goods rolling stock on the Danish State Railways is dark brown. For so relatively large a vehicle, measuring

38 ft. 6 in. over the buffers, the tare weight is surprisingly small, only 15½ tons, and it is designed to carry a pay-load of 17 tons. The refrigerant is water–ice, or solid carbon dioxide.

174 Iraqi State Railways: Double-decked Sheep Van.

The Iraqi State Railways, constructed as recently as between the years 1918 and 1941, traverses the historic land of Mesopotamia and consists of two distinct sections: a metre-gauge line running from the Persian Gulf, and following roughly the course of the River Euphrates to Baghdad, and a standard-gauge line running northwards from Baghdad through Mosul to the Turkish frontier at Tel Kotchek. It is over this latter route that a through passenger service is operated between Baghdad and Istanbul. The freight traffic, as on so many overseas railways nowadays, is, however, of much greater consequence than the passenger, and a number of thoroughly modern vehicles have been introduced for special duties. Our picture illustrates a high-capacity bogie van for carrying sheep. The loading gauge is liberal, and permits of two tiers for the animals. All rolling stock is fitted with continuous automatic brakes, but having regard to the nature of the country, speeds are not high. Even the through passenger trains between Baghdad and Tel Kotchek do not average more than 30 m.p.h. The sheep vans illustrated were built by the Birmingham Railway Carriage and Wagon Company.

175 Gold Coast Railways: The '221' Class Heavy Freight and Mineral 4–8–2 Locomotive.

After the end of the First World War considerable development took place in the Gold Coast (now Ghana) with a substantial increase in the mining industry, and to operate the heavy ore trains between Takoradi Harbour and Kumasi some powerful 4–8–2 locomotives were designed, and built by the Vulcan Foundry Ltd. These engines could be described as in the general traditions of Southern Africa at the time, with extremely long boilers. The maximum axle-load then permitted on this 3 ft. 6 in. gauge line was only 13 tons, and some careful designing was necessary to distribute the weight and provide adequate adhesion for a locomotive required to develop a tractive effort of some 30,000 lb. The boiler proper is, however, not of such an extreme length as it might appear, for between the front of the firebox and the firebox tubeplate there is a large combustion chamber. These locomotives were first introduced in 1924. They did good work on the heavy ore trains, and the Vulcan Foundry received a repeat order for 15 further engines of the class some years later. The principal dimensions were, cylinders 19¼ in. diameter by 24 in. stroke; coupled wheels 3 ft. 9 in. diameter; boiler pressure 180 lb. per sq. in.; total weight of engine and tender in working order 106½ tons. The tractive effort was 30,415 tons.

176 Italian State Railways: 2–6–0 Passenger Locomotive.

Locomotive practice in Italy has frequently presented many curious contradictions. In an earlier book of this series, dealing with railways at the turn of the century, the curious cab-in-front 0–6–4 tender engines of Signor Planchard were illustrated, while in very recent times we have become used to the curious spectacle of steam locomotives without chimneys, in the case of those fitted with the Franco-

Crosti boiler. The engine now illustrated is one of a numerous class of 2–6–0 having inside cylinders, but with the valve gear outside. This is an inversion of the more usual arrangement, but it was adopted on a few locomotives in England some fifty years ago, on the London and North Western Railway. The Italian 2–6–0s illustrated appeared to do their work very quietly and efficiently. They were much in evidence in the north-western part of the country on the lines between Milan and Turin, where they could be seen running fast with light trains.

177 Belgian National Railways: Semi-streamlined 'Pacific' Locomotive.

The distinguished record of locomotive design on the Belgian railways was notably continued in 1935 with the production of the striking new 'Pacific' shown in our picture. In outward appearance it bore a strong resemblance to the London and North Eastern *Cock o' the North* 2–8–2 as originally built, though the Belgian engine had four cylinders. There were originally 15 of the class, designed for heavy express passenger work. The four cylinders were $16\frac{1}{2}$ in. diameter by $28\frac{3}{8}$ in. stroke; coupled wheels 6 ft. 6 in. diameter, and the large boiler had 2527 sq. ft. of evaporative heating surface, superheater of 1202 sq. ft. and a grate area of 53·8 sq. ft. The firebox was exceptionally wide and had the unusual feature of having two firedoors, side by side. This made very hard work for the fireman, though none of the fast runs in Belgium was of very long duration, and the effort required, though severe, was short lived. The engine alone weighed 122 tons, and the very large tender with a water capacity of 10,560 gallons weighed no less than $82\frac{3}{4}$ tons when fully loaded.

The cylindrical accessories on the side of the boiler are those of the A.C.F.I. feedwater heater.

178 Hungarian State Railways: 4–8–0 Passenger Locomotive.

To British eyes the locomotives of Hungary must be among the ugliest on earth! They are, without exception, highly functional in appearance, with all fittings and appurtenances hung on outside, while the extreme height of the loading gauge enables them to be made exceptionally tall. These features are all epitomized in the large 4–8–0 locomotive shown in our picture. It is one of the series '424' class, and in steam days was the standard passenger engine of the country. Because of the extreme height of the boiler centre-line, a wide firebox could be readily accommodated well above the rearmost pairs of coupled wheels. They have coupled wheels 5 ft. 3 in. diameter, and two large cylinders 24 in. diameter by $26\frac{1}{2}$ in. stroke. All Hungarian locomotives are designed to steam freely on the poorest imaginable fuel. Frequently the tenders were loaded with a mixture of coal dust and briquettes, with a few wood blocks thrown in for good measure. The fact that the locomotives *did* steam, and successfully worked heavy trains, with this fuel is a tribute to the skill of the designers in proportioning boilers and fireboxes appropriately.

179 London and North Eastern Railway: The Class 'A4' 'Pacific' *Dwight D. Eisenhower*.

The Class 'A4' streamlined Pacifics of the L.N.E.R. first introduced by Sir Nigel Gresley in 1935 achieved instant and sensational success in high-speed running. The pioneer engine, the *Silver Link*, attained a speed of $112\frac{1}{2}$ m.p.h. within a few weeks of her completion at Doncaster Works, and in 1938 engine No. 4468 *Mallard* attained the world's record speed with steam, 126 m.p.h. In ordinary service the 'A4s' achieved a high degree of reliability. They were economical, and could haul very heavy trains, as well as running very swiftly with the high-speed streamliners. During the Second World War they were painted plain black, as an economy measure, and the deep valances of the original streamlined casing were taken off to facilitate maintenance. After the war the old livery of garter blue was restored on some of these famous engines, and No. 4496, originally named *Golden Shuttle* and used on the streamlined 'West Riding Limited' train, was renamed *Dwight D. Eisenhower* in honour of the victorious Allied Commander-in-Chief in Western Europe. After withdrawal from active service this engine was shipped to the U.S.A., and is now preserved there.

180 **London, Midland and Scottish Railway:** The 'Duchess' Class 'Pacific' of 1938.

Following experience with the 'Princess' class of 'Pacific' (ref. 110), it was felt desirable to have still greater boiler capacity. At the same time these 'Pacific' locomotives were closely approaching the maximum weight that could be permitted on the track. Some very careful design work was done on the boiler, using special lightweight alloy steels and improved construction techniques, and an increase in total heating surface from 2967 to 3637 sq. ft., and an increase in grate area from 45 to 50 sq. ft. was contrived, while adding only $\frac{3}{4}$ ton to the total weight of the engine—

$104\frac{1}{2}$ to $105\frac{1}{4}$ tons. With certain refinements also in the steam circuit the 'Duchess' class became the finest express passenger locomotive to run in Great Britain. Like the 'Princess' class which preceded them, they had four cylinders, and carried a boiler pressure of 250 lb. per sq. in. A number of them were at first streamlined; but this feature was eventually found not to be necessary, and the normally styled locomotives, as shown in our picture, were easily capable of speeds in excess of 100 m.p.h.

181 **Paris–Orléans–Midi Railway:** The Chapelon 4–8–0 (Rebuilt from 4–6–2).

This remarkable engine, which must be considered alongside the famous Chapelon 'Pacific' (ref. 44), was a further product of the modernization programme for locomotives launched in the 1930s by Monsieur André Chapelon. The 4–8–0 was a rebuild of an earlier Pacific design with smaller wheels than the high-speed main-line engines, and the 4–8–0 was produced for working over the heavy gradients of the Central France line. With the numerous aids to efficiency packed into the rebuilt engines some astonishing performances were put up. In relation to the size and weight of the locomotive they have never been surpassed. The use of these rebuilt engines was extended from the Paris–Orléans to the Paris, Lyons, and Mediterranean line with equally brilliant results. Unfortunately the locomotives *were* rebuilds, using the chassis of the original Pacifics, and the frame construction could not stand indefinitely the transmission of power more than double that for which it was originally designed. These magnificent engines therefore had a relatively short life in their rebuilt form, and were withdrawn shortly after the Second World War.

182 New York Central Lines: The 'Niagara' 4-8-4 High-speed Locomotive.

By the outbreak of the Second World War the diesel–electric locomotive was making rapid headway in America. The claims of more intense utilization, higher thermal efficiency, and cleanliness were being pressed with ever-increasing vigour, yet on many railroads the administrations were not convinced that the ultimate in steam had yet been reached. Certainly this was so on the New York Central, and the magnificent 'Niagara' class was designed to achieve with steam all that was claimed for the diesels. They were built by the American Locomotive Company in 1945, and designed to haul express trains of 20 coaches (about 1200 tons) at 85 m.p.h. on level track. The cylinders were $25\frac{1}{2}$ in. diameter by 32 in. stroke; coupled wheels 6 ft. 7 in. diameter, and tractive effort 61,570 lb. The tender, which carried 41 tons of coal, was nearly as heavy as the engine, 188 tons, against 210 tons. The tremendously hard work they performed in working throughout over the 930 miles between Harmon and Chicago involved refuelling *en route*, despite the huge tenders, and on the heaviest and fastest trains it was not unusual to burn more than 100 tons of coal on one journey!

183 London, Midland and Scottish Railway: The Stanier 'Turbomotive'.

In the mid-1930s, when so much development was taking place in railway motive power, deep consideration was given to alternative means of steam traction, and the non-condensing turbine 'Pacific' locomotive introduced by Sir William Stanier on the London, Midland and Scottish Railway was one outcome of this trend. It was built to compete with the reciprocating steam 'Pacific' of the 'Princess Royal' class (ref. 110), and did very well in a lengthy series of trials between London and Glasgow. In ordinary service it worked between London and Liverpool. Over a number of years regular running the overall efficiency showed a small improvement upon the performance of the ordinary 'Pacific' engines, though the machinery was subject at times to failure, which caused the locomotive to be out of service for months at a time. The eventual verdict, reached after many years of experimental and regular running, was that the special nature of the machinery and the cost of maintaining it, was not justified by the relatively small improvement in overall efficiency, and in the early 1950s the locomotive was reconstructed as a reciprocating Pacific.

184 Great Northern Railway of U.S.A.: A 4000-horse-power Diesel-Electric Express Locomotive.

At the end of this book it is appropriate to provide a glimpse of the new age, and nowhere more fitting than in the U.S.A., where the diesel locomotive made its most rapid early progress. The earlier General Motors standard type, consisting of 2000-horsepower units, was supplied to many American railroads, and their introduction was accompanied by the adoption of gay new colours. The Great Northern style was one of the most vivid, and the locomotive illustrated, comprising two of the standard 2000-horsepower units, was in very common use during the latter part of the Second World War and during the time when such intensive propaganda was being issued for the replacement of steam. Some very high availabilities were claimed for the new power, such as 95 per cent as compared with 60 per cent for the very latest steam; but such remarkable utilization was not frequently sustained over a lengthy period. Nevertheless, locomotives like this Great Northern example ushered in the new age of railway traction, and deserve a notable place in history.

BIBLIOGRAPHY

BOOKS

L. M. Vilain, *Les Locomotives à vapeur Françaises du 'Type Pacific'*, Vigot Frères, Paris, 1959

A Century of Locomotives, New South Wales, 1855–1955, A. H. R. S., Angus and Robertson, 1961

O. S. Nock, *Southern Steam*, David and Charles, 1966

O. S. Nock, *L.N.E.R. Steam*, David and Charles, 1969

L. G. Marshall, *Steam on the R.E.N.F.E.*, Macmillan, 1965

O. S. Nock, *Fifty Years of Railway Signalling*, Ian Allan, 1965

A. N. Palmer and W. W. Stewart, *Calvalcade of New Zealand Locomotives*, Angus & Robertson, 1961

P. Ransome-Wallis (Editor), *The Concise Encyclopaedia of World Railway Locomotives*, Hutchinson, 1959

L. J. Harrigan, *Victoria Railways to '62*, Victorian Railways, Melbourne, 1962

J. N. Westwood, *Soviet Railways Today*, Ian Allan, 1963

Jane's World Railways, Sampson Low, 1968–69

Vulcan Locomotives, Vulcan Foundry

Beyer Garratt Locomotives, Beyer, Peacock and Co. Ltd.

PERIODICALS

The Railway Magazine, Transport and Technical Publications
The Railway Gazette, Transport and Technical Publications
The Railway Engineer, Transport and Technical Publications
Baldwins Locomotives
Modern Railways, Modern Transport Publication Co. Ltd.

INDEX